STRONG WOMEN

STRONG WOMEN

15 Biographies of
INFLUENTIAL WOMEN
HISTORY OVERLOOKED

Kari Koeppel

ROCKRIDGE
PRESS

For general information on our other products and services or to obtain technical support, please contact our Customer Care Department within the United States at (866) 744-2665, or outside the United States at (510) 253-0500.

Rockridge Press publishes its books in a variety of electronic and print formats. Some content that appears in print may not be available in electronic books, and vice versa.

Interior and Cover Designer: Erin Yeung
Art Producer: Hannah Dickerson
Editor: Morgan Shanahan
Production Manager: Martin Worthington
Production Editor: Sigi Nacson

Illustrations © 2020 Roberta Oriano

Author photo courtesy of Caitlin Cowie

ISBN: Print 978-1-64611-685-0 | eBook 978-1-64611-686-7

R0

To my parents, who always thought
I would do something literary.

Contents

Introduction

Choosing the women to include in this book was far more difficult than I ever could have anticipated. As a professional researcher, I've spent my career going down rabbit holes of information, often about incredible women, many of whom were lost to—or erased from—history. So, the chance to highlight all these stories in a single book? It was a dream project; I couldn't wait to discover and share the incredible strength exhibited by women through-out history. I had no idea just how deep the imprint of women on all aspects of human advancement truly is. That's how much the patriarchy-written history has brainwashed even a self-described feminist like me: I was blown away to discover amazing women left and right in every time period, subject, and area of the world I looked. When my list had grown to more than 200 women, I had to draw a line, but I knew there were so many more women to discover. I could keep researching forever and never finish. The guilt crept in as I narrowed down my list to just 15 women. The overwhelming scale of the feats of women almost became desen-sitizing. I found myself thinking things like, *Ah, she won a Nobel Prize, but aside from that, she isn't very interesting. Yes, she was the first woman in Japan to receive a bachelor of science degree, but she didn't do much afterward.* Wait, what? Who did I think I was? Each and every woman I'd discovered had accomplished incredible things against all odds and deserved her rightful place in the history books.

But I had a page limit and a deadline keeping me from writing the encyclopedia I could so easily have filled, and I had to select just 15. After several rounds of excruciating cuts, I finally settled on these truly stellar women, and I'm honored and thrilled to share them with you. I'm hopeful that this book will be a gateway to telling more women's stories.

What I learned from these 15 women is that ordinary women are extraordinary, and they always have been. Our society is richly textured and layered with so much history that many of us don't take the time to understand or marvel at. For many of these women, their extraordinary actions could boil down to the post-9/11 credo, "If you see something, say something." If something is wrong, unfair, or unjust—say something. It's as simple and scary as that. Years ago, I read an interview with writer and director Lena Dunham in which she relayed advice her father had given her: "Go where there's a 'you-shaped' hole in the world." That has always stuck with me, and I kept thinking about it as I wrote about these women. The you-shaped hole was not always obvious. Sometimes they squeezed into a tiny opening, and it became you-shaped after the fact. But that space allowed other women climb through after them.

Women did not suddenly start advocating for themselves and making massive contributions to society in the 20th century. The 20th century is simply when the stranglehold of the patriarchy eased and women gained more freedom and legal rights to independence from their husbands and fathers. Did you know women weren't allowed to apply for their own credit card or bank loan without a mail cosignor until *1974*? Even today, married couples get certain benefits—tax breaks, insurance cuts—that make life easier and less expensive. What purpose could the government have to incentivize marriage apart from encouraging women to tie themselves to men? This is one of the reasons legalizing same-sex marriage was so important. I don't think US government officials sat down one day and said, "You know, we'd like to subjugate women. What's a good way of doing that?" After thousands of years of subjugation, maybe men didn't even think it was an option for a woman to be treated as a whole person. The Constitution labeled black men as counting as three-fifths of a person. Abigail Adams (a candidate for this book who didn't make the cut) famously wrote to her husband, John Adams, while he was at the Constitutional Congress, "I desire you would Remember the Ladies, and be more generous and favourable to them than your ancestors. Do not put such unlimited power into the hands of Husbands. Remember all Men would be tyrants if they could." And yet, I don't see the ladies mentioned anywhere in that original document. Purposeful subjugation is *real*, people.

Some of the women included in this book had the courage to stand up to the law and work to amend the law to make it fairer. Following the law is not always the moral thing to do.

The quieting of women and their innate power is easily accomplished by simply letting their stories fade away. However valuable the accomplishments of women may be to society, time and again women themselves are deemed inconsequential. And the historical record reflects that. When white men predominantly shape the collective history as we know it, everyone else falls to the wayside. Other voices aren't deemed valuable. But we can correct the record by bringing to light the facts as best as they've been preserved and celebrating the people who took risks and created you-shaped holes for the rest of us. We can insert the names of unsung heroines into the pages of history books and make them household names. Ultimately, this book is about that hope.

Much has been made in recent years about representation: If you see it, you believe it. If you see someone like you doing something, you believe it's an option for you to do the same. In writing the women documented here out of history, other women were kept from seeing them and believing they, too, could be a doctor, a detective, or an army commander. Maybe it didn't even occur to women that they could question the lanes they were told to stay in. My hope is that in excavating these 15 stories, we can prove that women have always been well rounded, complicated, complete humans with ambitions, beliefs, courage, and a deep-rooted sense of survival. And while that need to survive kept them in roles the patriarchy prescribed, sometimes that preservation instinct took the form of fighting against some of the greatest evils in history.

*Together we are powerful, and we have a
seldom-told, seldom-remembered history
of victories and transformations that give
us confidence that, yes, we can change the
world because we have many times before.*

—Rebecca Solnit, "Grounds for Hope," foreword to
the third edition of *Hope in the Dark* (2015)

PART ONE

THE INNOVATORS

History, for the most part, was written by men, who cemented their own accomplishments—leaving out the women who'd paved the way alongside them (or even ahead of them). The omission of the contributions of women from the historical record created a narrative that incorrectly placed men at the forefront of innovation. It's time to correct the record.

MURASAKI SHIKIBU

(c. 973–c. 1014)

Murasaki Shikibu was born into an aristocratic family in 10th-century Japan, when an education was not considered necessary for a girl. Murasaki didn't let social norms stand in her way. She went on to write what many consider the most influential work in all of Japanese literature. Although she should be a household name, Murasaki's given name has been left out of history, and we know her only by a sobriquet.

The recorded details of Murasaki's life are limited. We know her father was a scholar and provincial governor born into a minor branch of the powerful Fujiwara family, which ruled Japan from behind the scenes between the 9th and 12th centuries. Murasaki was born around 973 in Kyoto, Japan. She reportedly learned Chinese—at that time the dominant language of the Japanese government and traditionally taught only to men—by eavesdropping on her father's lessons with her brother. She studied works by Chinese writers and became a well-read young woman at a time when girls were usually not educated. She likely accompanied her governor father to his different postings, including Echizen, north of Kyoto, in 996.

During this period, women's names were generally not recorded, and the author's real name is unknown. Murasaki comes from the name of a character in her novel, *The Tale of Genji*. She is the main love interest of the story's protagonist, who may have been autobiographical, and Shikibu relates to the position her father held.

Murasaki was married around 999 to a much older, wealthy courtier who was possibly a distant cousin in the Fujiwara clan (political control was exerted via strategic marriages and diplomacy). She may not have been his only wife, as it was common, even expected, for aristocratic men to have several wives and concubines. Murasaki's husband died just a few years into their marriage, but not before she gave birth to a child, likely a daughter. Around 1006, Murasaki was summoned to court to serve as a lady-in-waiting to the Empress Shoshi. Murasaki was likely chosen because of her literary skills, which would have been highly valued at court. Her family didn't rank high enough for her to be there for any reason other than merit. Scholars have debated whether she had begun to write and circulate *The Tale of Genji* following her husband's death, but the exact timeline is lost to history. Her diary, however, survived, and provides the most insight into just who Murasaki was.

According to a 14th-century legend about Murasaki Shikibu, she created *The Tale of Genji* after the empress asked her to write a story. The legend claims that Murasaki went on a journey to the

Ishiyama-dera temple near Lake Biwa, east of Kyoto, searching for inspiration. That night, staring out over the lake underneath a full moon, she dreamed up the story she would write. In 1920 the Houghton Mifflin Company published fragments of a diary Murasaki kept during her time as a lady in waiting from late 1008 to early 1010. Her diary contains poetry, as does *The Tale of Genji*, but Murasaki also recorded how the culture of superficiality and politics made her feel out of place in the royal court, and that keeping her distance gave her the perspective from which to write about it. Still, she was close with the empress, and gave her secret lessons in reading classic Chinese poetry. Murasaki staged readings of *The Tale of Genji* for the empress with accompanying pictures, which was how stories were typically told at court at the time. The female narrator of the novel appears to be addressing a superior, possibly a clue that the story was written to entertain the empress. Murasaki is thought to have completed *The Tale of Genji* around 1010, although estimates range from 1005 to 1014. She may have given these readings before completing the work, instead presenting chapters as they were finished. Both men and women at court read printings of the novel, which was very unusual because *Genji* was written in Japanese and the men at court read mainly in Chinese.

The Tale of Genji consists of 54 chapters, with modern English translations running more than 1,000 pages. The first 41 chapters center on the life of Genji, a prince so handsome he is nicknamed "the Shining Prince" and is described at age 17 as "so beautiful that one could have wished him a woman." He's the son of an emperor, but his mother is of a lower birth, so he won't succeed the throne. The plot generally follows Genji's many romantic adventures. In some ways, Genji is a forerunner to Don Juan or Casanova. Each woman he encounters is described in vivid detail—and they are more likely to be complimented for their gentleness or calligraphy skills than praised for their physical beauty. And although seduction is the primary goal in most of Genji's interactions, some of the emotional relationships feel modern in their sensitivity and complexity. Genji's great love is Murasaki (from whom the author's sobriquet is taken), whose common birth means she can't be

Genji's main wife, even though he wants her to be. Despite the narrative's focus on Genji's sexual trysts, he is destroyed by Murasaki's death and dies soon afterward.

The final 14 chapters of *The Tale of Genji* take place eight years after the prince's death and center on Kaoru, thought to be Genji's son, and Niou, Genji's grandson (from different wives). The tone becomes much darker, and the book ends abruptly. Scholars have debated whether this was the author's intention or if a final chapter has been lost. Additionally, the sharp change in tone has led some to contest the authorship of the final 14 chapters. Some theorize that *The Tale of Genji* had multiple authors and suggest it was finished after Murasaki's death. There's no evidence that anyone other than Murasaki Shikibu wrote the novel, and she mentions its existence in her diary, but no original copies of the manuscript remain. The oldest version known to exist is thought to have been made around 1200 by a court poet named Fujiwara no Teika.

Women's names were generally not recorded, and the author's real name is unknown. Murasaki comes from the name of a character in her novel, *The Tale of Genji*. She is the main love interest of the story's protagonist, who may have been autobiographical, and Shikibu relates to the position her father held.

Murasaki is last mentioned in a record from 1013, and it's thought she passed away the following year.

The Tale of Genji was an immediate hit at court, and its influence on Japanese art and literature has been enormous. It may be the most influential work in the country's literary history. Certainly, it was the standard against which all future Japanese literature was judged. *The Tale of Genji* has been the subject of countless books and articles of literary analysis, and numerous philosophers have studied it extensively. Murasaki has served as a model for other women writers in the 1,000 years since the epic was written. The book was first translated to English by Arthur Waley in 1925. Upon its release, Virginia Woolf reviewed it for British *Vogue*, writing, "Story after story flows from the brush of Murasaki." Critics from less hedonistic eras of Japanese culture looked down on Genji's behavior, with women praying for Murasaki's soul, but still revered her artistic work; eras with similar values made Genji even more core to its culture. In the Edo period (1603–1868), it was common for prostitutes to name themselves after Genji's many lovers.

Immediately following the book's completion, *The Tale of Genji* and its author became popular subjects in Japanese visual art. For more than 1,000 years, artists have created paintings, pottery, scrolls, folding screens, and fabric art depicting *Genji*'s characters, stories, and legends, as well as Murasaki in the act of writing. In recent years, exhibitions at major art museums like the Metropolitan Museum of Art in New York have centered on this artistic tradition. In 2008, Kyoto marked the book's 1,000-year anniversary with celebrations throughout the city.

ALICE GUY-BLACHÉ

(1873–1968)

Many would say, and few would argue, that filmmaking has a gender problem. But what if history told us this wasn't always the case? In the early days of filmmaking, the male-to-female ratio wasn't in such stark contrast. Before Hollywood diversity reports, and before a film Academy predominately populated by older white men, women like Alice Guy-Blaché helped create the movie industry.

Alice Guy was born on July 1, 1873, in the Parisian suburb of Saint-Mandé to French-Chilean parents Marie and Émile Guy. Her mother was born and raised in France but was married off to her father, a book merchant, who was an acquaintance of her aunt and uncle in Chile and from a French family. Alice was the fifth and youngest child and the only one born in France. Not long after Alice's birth, her parents returned to Chile, leaving her in the care of her maternal grandmother for three years. By the time her mother came back to retrieve her in France, Alice had completely forgotten her.

Arriving in Chile with her mother, Alice met her father for the first time. She spent the next two years in the care of a Chilean caretaker, Conchita, while her parents busied themselves with their own affairs. Her father took her back to France at age 6 to enroll her in the same boarding school as her sisters. She had forgotten French while in Chile and had to relearn it. She attended the school for six years before a series of earthquakes in Chile resulted in financial problems for her parents. Her father returned to France to move the girls to a less expensive school when, tragically, Alice's older brother died suddenly at age 17 from a rheumatic heart. Her mother then joined the family in France. As Alice was finishing her education, her father passed away. With two of her sisters married and the other still in school, it was up to Alice to support her mother.

At the advice of one of her mother's friends, Alice took stenography lessons to boost her chances of securing employment. She soon got a secretarial job at a factory, where one of her male colleagues verbally harassed her. Alice stood up to him and remained at the factory. When she learned of a new secretarial role opening up at the Comptoir general de Photographie in 1894, she was intrigued. She interviewed for the position with Léon Gaumont, who hired her based on her dictation skills. Alice quickly got up to speed on the camera equipment and earned Gaumont's trust. After a short time, she was promoted to office manager. The following year, Gaumont purchased the Comptoir and renamed the company Gaumont.

In December 1895, Gaumont and Alice were invited to attend a presentation by Auguste and Louis Lumière, Gaumont's colleagues and rivals in the camera business. On December 28, 1895, the Lumière brothers showed the audience, including Alice, the first motion picture film, *Exiting the Factory*. This showing sparked a race to develop this new medium. Films showed off the technology and depicted simple slice-of-life scenes.

Alice thought these films would be more interesting if there was a narrative. In 1896, she asked Gaumont if she could make a couple of short films of her own. He thought it was a "silly, girlish thing to do," but he agreed on the condition that her filmmaking would not interfere with her secretarial duties. Alice wrote a scenario, had a set built, and hired her friends as actors. She shot *La Fée aux Choux* ("The Cabbage Fairy"), a one-minute film about a woman going shopping for a baby in a cabbage patch. Alice was 22 and had just directed what was likely the first fictional film. She had also just fallen in love. She later wrote in her memoir, "Permit me to present to you the one who has filled my life entirely . . . my own Prince Charming. The Cinema."

Gaumont named Alice head of film production at the company, and she set into motion a period of experimentation. Alice and her collaborators—all male, many of whom went on to illustrious film careers—shot on the streets of Paris. They originated the close-up shot; hand-painted the film to add color; used special effects like films reversed, slowed down, accelerated, or double-exposed; and synchronized sound through Gaumont's new innovation, the Chronophone. The Chronophone had a wax recording device that played sound in sync with images, which enabled actors to record sound ahead of time, then mouth their lines along with the recording. Alice was the only director at the company until 1905, when her success required the hiring of additional directors. She directed approximately 600 films for Gaumont, including more than 100 sound films.

The majority of Alice's films were one to two minutes long; however, as time went on and she gained experience, the length and depth of her films increased. Notable was her 30-minute *La Vie du Christ* (1906), which had more than 300 extras. Alice made films of every genre, and they were always scripted. A story in Alice's memoir describes an early showing of one of her comedies, during which a woman twisted around in her seat, laughing hysterically, and begged, "Enough, Enough, I'll make pipi!" Alice also noted, however, "Comedy is much more difficult than drama."

Gaumont's success turned it into an international company. One of its English employees, Herbert Blaché-Bolton, came to France to shadow Alice and her crew. He wanted to learn their methods so he could take a position as assistant manager of the Gaumont branch in Berlin. Herbert was raised in England, educated in France, and hired for his skill with language. Alice and Herbert went to film a bullfight in the south of France, and on the trip they fell in love. Upon returning to Paris, Herbert left for his post in Berlin. As fate would have it, Alice was soon sent to Berlin for work and they were reunited. They decided that unless their feelings changed, they would be engaged at Christmas. A few days before Christmas, Herbert arrived in Paris with his English father to formally ask for Alice's hand in marriage.

> "Permit me to present to you the one who has filled my life entirely . . . my own Prince Charming. The Cinema."

Alice had said about marriage, "I suppose that I love my work too much. If I decide someday to marry, it will only be to have children." She and Herbert were married in 1907. Alice was 33 years old. The couple immediately set off for the United States, as Gaumont had sold its patents for the Chronophone to two American entrepreneurs in Cleveland, Ohio. Alice resigned from her role at Gaumont, presumably with the intention of giving up her career for a traditional role as a wife and mother. Upon the couple's arrival in the United States, they dropped Bolton from their last name; instead, they were Herbert Blaché and Alice Guy-Blaché. Alice spoke no English when she arrived, but she picked it up quickly. After nine months, the new owners made no movement on the Chronophone, so the patent reverted to Gaumont, who was then in Long Island, New York, opening a studio in Flushing. Gaumont invited Herbert to manage the studio, so he and Alice moved to New York.

In 1908, Alice gave birth to their first child—a daughter, Simone. But she couldn't resist the lure of the studio and decided to resume filmmaking. In 1910, she started her own film company, Solax, of which she was president and chief director, making her the first woman studio head. Herbert was contracted with Gaumont, so he wasn't officially involved, but Solax was located on the lot next to Gaumont and they worked on scenarios together. They made a series of cowboy films first, followed by military films. Alice's pace was no slower than it had been at Gaumont in Paris, although her films had grown longer. By 1912, Solax was so successful that the company built a new studio in Fort Lee, New Jersey, which was the center of the film world. Alice hung a sign in her studio featuring her motto for her actors: Be Natural. That same year, Alice gave birth to their second child, a son named Reginald. The press loved Alice; she wrote in her memoir, "I rarely passed a week without being interviewed."

Around this time, Herbert completed his contract with Gaumont and took over as president of Solax. Alice claimed she was happy to give up the business aspect and focus on the creative side. The film industry was shifting, however, thanks to the Lumière and Gaumont patents entering the public domain, and under Herbert's leadership, Solax stumbled. By early 1914, Solax was out of business. Historians have speculated that Herbert was jealous of Alice and Solax would always have been associated with her success. In late 1913, overlapping with the demise of Solax, Herbert founded a new company: Blaché Features. Blaché's films shot on the Solax stages and used many of the same actors. Alice and Herbert traded off directing duties, but Alice's films were generally better received. They received an offer to buy their company for $200,000 in shares with a directing contract for $600,000 for the couple, but they declined. Blaché Features didn't last long. World War I made the costs of running a studio unfeasible, and the company shuttered.

Coinciding with the collapse of Blaché Features, both of Alice's children came down with the measles. She took them to the North

Carolina coast to recover, and Herbert ran off to California with one of his leading ladies. Alice came back to New York determined to make a living. She put her children in boarding school and set out to direct-for-hire. In 1919, while directing a film, she caught the Spanish flu during the deadly epidemic. She was still quite sick when Herbert came to visit. He asked her to come to California with the children (as Alice wrote in her memoir, "I believe my sad look moved him"). It's unclear whether he had any intention of getting back together with Alice, but when she arrived in Los Angeles, they lived separately.

In Los Angeles, which was now the center of the film industry, Alice tried to revive her film career. She found that while people in the industry remembered and celebrated her, they had moved on. To earn money, she often worked as Herbert's assistant director, a role reversal that likely didn't help studio heads see her as a viable director. She wanted to make a film with Charlie Chaplin, whom she'd met back in New York, but he was filming *The Kid* (1921) and told her he preferred to improvise rather than work with a script. Alice directed two more features for Metro Pictures. They were her last.

Herbert and Alice officially divorced in 1920. Around the same time, Alice received a letter from her lawyer requesting that she return to Fort Lee and sort through what remained of the Solax/Blaché studio, as Herbert was ignoring the matter. While she oversaw the auctioning off of the plant, she was invited to direct *Tarzan of the Apes* on the condition that she invest $50,000 in the business. But Alice didn't have the money, so she lost the opportunity. She decided to return to France with Simone and Reginald, and they settled in Nice with her sister. She attempted to find work in the French film industry but had no luck. Her divorce from Herbert had granted her a small alimony, which he had stopped paying because of the declining world economy, and she gradually sold off her belongings to support her children. After 10 years in Nice, the family moved to Paris, where Simone and Reginald, both now grown, found work.

During Alice's time in France, she was written out of film history and watched as many of her films were credited to her male competitors. Meanwhile, Lois Weber was credited as the first woman director, although she was actually the first American woman to direct a movie. Alice decided to start writing her memoirs as a means of correcting history. When Simone got a job at the American embassy in Switzerland at the start of World War II, Alice moved with her. After the war, in 1952, Simone was transferred to Washington, DC, and the family returned to the States. Alice began looking for copies of her films, including at the Library of Congress, but there was no sign of them. Films in those days, especially in the early Gaumont era, were not carefully archived—it was an entirely new field, so how could they have known?—and the nitrate film itself was wildly flammable.

When Alice and Simone returned to Paris in 1955, thanks to the efforts of Gaumont's son Louis, Alice was honored with the French Legion of Honor, an award celebrating her pioneering film career. This honor brought her back from obscurity, and she began giving interviews to set the record straight. She was still working on her memoirs at the age of 90 when she suffered a stroke. Alice still lived with Simone, who never married and had retired, and they moved back to New Jersey in 1964. After a bad fall caused Alice's health to deteriorate rapidly, Simone put her in a nursing home, where she passed away on March 24, 1968, at age 94.

At the time of Alice's death, only four of her films had been recovered. Fifty years later, about 150 of the nearly 1,000 films she directed had been found, including one with an all-black cast. Her memoirs were published in France in 1976, and 10 years later in the United States with a translation by Simone. Film scholars have rediscovered Alice's oeuvre, renewing her place in history. Martin Scorsese described her as "a filmmaker of rare sensitivity with a remarkably poetic eye." Museums like New York's Museum of Modern Art and the Whitney have done retrospectives of her work, and a documentary about her life, *Be Natural,* was released in 2019. Alice's gravestone in Mahwah, New Jersey, was updated in 2012 to note that she was the first woman film director, first woman studio head, and president of Solax.

ADA LOVELACE

(1815–1852)

Ada Lovelace was born into a family of nobility, privilege, and plenty of scandal, but her story has long been overshadowed by that of her father, poet Lord Byron. And yet every day around the globe, her contributions to modern technology are evident. While Regency-era England is often associated with such incredible women as Jane Austen and Mary Shelley, the period might be the last place you'd expect to find the woman considered the world's first computer programmer.

Born Augusta Ada Byron on December 10, 1815, just outside London, Ada was the only legitimate child of the infamous poet Lord Byron. Her mother, Annabella Milbanke, was an heiress and mathematics enthusiast whom Lord Byron once called the "Princess of Parallelograms." It was a bit of a backhanded compliment, as the accolade highlighted their divergent lifestyles. Lord and Lady Byron had not been married a year when his scandalous life caught up with them and she left him, taking one-month-old Ada with her. Lord Byron soon left England, and Ada never saw her father again. He died eight years later in Greece.

Lady Byron was determined that Ada would be nothing like her father. She carefully curated Ada's education from an early age, focusing on math and science and steering her away from poetry. Lady Byron initially taught Ada herself, emphasizing how to think rather than how to memorize; she also showed Ada the practical applications of concepts she was learning. Ada reportedly began to learn the alphabet at age 2, and by age 6 she had a governess who oversaw her daily studies in reading, grammar, spelling, arithmetic, music, geography, drawing, and French. Lady Byron was a hypochondriac and traveled frequently. Ada wrote to her mother every day, even when she was at home. Ada's governess soon added history, literature, chemistry, shorthand, algebra, geometry, and sewing to her curriculum.

When Ada was 11, Lady Byron took her on a yearlong tour of Europe. When Ada returned, she developed an obsession with the concept of flying. She wanted to figure out a way to create wings, or a flying machine, and studied bird anatomy and mechanics, calling the study "flyology." Her concepts were a marriage between the mathematical skill and big-picture thinking her mother had taught her and the wild, genius creativity she had inherited from her father. At age 13, Ada got sick with measles and didn't fully recover until three years later, but her studies continued. Her mother sought the advice of famed scientist Mary Somerville regarding Ada's education.

In June 1833, 17-year-old Ada went through the upper-class ritual of being presented at court and introduced into high society. She met 41-year-old widower and scientist Charles Babbage, purportedly through an introduction by Mary Somerville. The two clicked, and he invited Ada and Lady Byron to see the recently completed prototype of his "Difference Engine," a computational machine designed to reduce the labor of creating mathematical tables. For a girl who had been taught to appreciate practical applications of math and science since birth, Babbage's machine was a revelation. He had been working on the Difference Engine for more than a decade and had received funding from the British government to create it, but while he was passionate about designs and theories, he did a poor job of managing the engineers hired to actually build it. He told Ada about his ideas for the "Analytical Engine," the next step in his dream of mechanized computation. They began a correspondence about their mathematical ambitions that lasted for the rested of Ada's life.

Two years later, Ada met and married Lord William King, who later became Earl of Lovelace (and thus Lord Lovelace per British titling conventions). Ada was 19; he was 30. She quickly had three children: Byron (named for her father) in 1836, Annabella (named for her mother) in 1837, and Ralph in 1839. Soon after Ralph's birth, Ada wrote to Babbage that she wanted to resume her study of mathematics. He introduced her to Augustus de Morgan, a mathematics professor at University College London, who taught her advanced mathematics, including calculus. He later told Lady Byron that if Ada were a man, she would have been a prominent mathematician. Ada was more interested in her studies than the more socially accepted role of doting mother. In 1841, she wrote to Lady Byron, "I believe myself to possess a most singular combination of qualities exactly fitted to make me preeminently a discoverer of the hidden realities of nature." The same year, however, her health took a turn for the worse, and she was prescribed opiates for her pain.

Meanwhile, Charles Babbage had traveled to Turin, Italy, to lecture on the Analytical Engine, during which a 30-year-old army engineer named Luigi Menabrea took notes. In October 1842, Menabrea, who would later become the Italian Prime Minister, published a paper written in French on Babbage's lectures. Babbage suggested that Ada write her own paper on the Analytical Engine, but by February 1843, she decided to translate Menabrea's paper to English instead. Mary Somerville had taken a similar path to science by starting with a translation of a foreign work. Ada was determined to add her own thoughts and analysis on the Analytical Engine at the end of her translation. She worked on the translation and her notes over the course of nine months and corresponded with Babbage almost daily—sometimes multiple times a day—with messages carried via courier or the postal service (at that time, mail in London was delivered six times a day). It was almost like a modern-day work email thread: Ada would ask questions, Babbage would answer; Babbage would make a request, Ada would respond; Ada would send drafts, Babbage would comment. She wrapped up her work in July 1843, and Babbage requested that he be allowed to write an anonymous preface blasting the British government for failing to finance the project. Ada refused.

Ada's seven notes at the end of her translation, listed A through G, were far longer than the translation itself, and they clearly explained how the Analytical Engine would work. She compared the engine to the Jacquard loom, a silk-weaving machine that used punched cards to create elaborate patterns. In Note G, Ada laid out a plan to use punched cards to perform a sequence of Bernoulli numbers, and in doing so created what is considered today to be the first computer program. Her work on the program is documented in letters to Babbage describing the challenges she faced: "My Dear Babbage. I am in much dismay at having got into so amazing a quagmire & botheration with these Numbers, that I cannot possibly get the thing done today. . . . I am now going out on horseback." Her work was a huge innovation: Ada saw past simple computation and predicted the possibility of creation via programmed instructions.

Ada's translation was published in 1843. She was proud of her work and sent copies to her mother, writing, "This is a pleasant prospect for the future, as I suppose many hundreds & thousands of such formulae will come forth from my pen." Ada's husband was just as proud, and he sent copies to friends. In Ada's mind, this was the first step in a long and beautiful career in the sciences.

Between completing her notes and the publication of her paper, Ada proposed to Babbage that she take over the project management duties for building the Analytical Engine. Her husband supported the idea. She anxiously awaited Babbage's response, writing to him again the next day when she hadn't heard from him. He eventually answered, initially refusing the offer, but he soon relented and gave her his blessing.

Lady Anne Blunt
(1837–1917)

Ada Lovelace's daughter, Lady Anne Blunt, traveled extensively in the Middle East with her husband, becoming the first European woman to do so. They brought Arabian horses back to England, and today more than 90 percent of the world's Arabian horses are said to be descended from them. She wrote two books on the Middle East and eventually moved to Egypt full time, where she died in 1917.

After the publication of her notes and translation, Ada focused on raising her children and went through another period of bad health. By the time she recovered, she'd moved on to other scientific interests. She wanted to write "a Calculus of the Nervous System," but it never materialized. This was partly because, as a woman, she couldn't gain access to the Royal Society's library but also because she continued to suffer from poor health.

In the mid-1840s, Ada began an affair with the amateur scientist John Crosse. Their romance was seemingly fueled by similar intellectual interests. When Ada died, she left John Crosse her writing box to remind him of their "many delightful and improving hours" together. Few details are known of their affair because Ada's husband bought and destroyed all her correspondence from Crosse for £600 (about $110,000 today); however, Crosse apparently remained in Ada's life in some capacity until she died.

Lady Byron remained an overbearing figure in Ada's life. In 1847, Ada's two youngest children, Annabella and Ralph, went to live with their grandmother. Perhaps in the search for fun and freedom that she hadn't experienced in her youth, Ada developed a fondness for gambling on horse racing. This took a toll: By 1851, she had reportedly run up thousands of pounds in debt.

Before the issue could come to a head, Ada's health again took a dive. This time, she did not recover. Her physician, Dr. Locock, believed that illnesses, especially terminal ones, shouldn't be disclosed to the patient until absolutely necessary; he thought hinting at the diagnosis would give the patient time to adjust to the idea of death. In June 1851, Dr. Locock told Ada's husband that she had cancer on the "neck and mouth of the womb." Historians debate whether that meant uterine or cervical cancer. He told Ada that her condition was "perfectly curable" with rest and time.

By July 1852, Ada realized—mainly through cues she picked up from her friends and family—she wasn't going to get better. She was in a lot of pain that only increased as her disease worsened. Around this time Ada's mother became more involved with her daily care. Ostensibly concerned for her daughter's soul, Lady Byron pressed Ada to contemplate death and make a deathbed repentance of her sins. Ada, who was not very religious for most of her life, was worn down by her long illness, increasing pain, and the effects of the opiates she took to manage her discomfort. Lady Byron controlled who Ada saw, turning away everyone, including Charles Babbage. Ada's health severely deteriorated at the end of August. On September 1, Ada was compelled to confess her affair with John Crosse to Lord Lovelace, who was upset by the news. Ada held on for a few more months and died on November 27, 1852. She was only 36 years old—the same age as Lord Byron when he died, although Ada outlived him by several months.

At Ada's request, she was buried in the Byron family vault next to her father—reunited with him for the first time since birth. Lady Byron hated the idea, but built a memorial to Ada with a sonnet Ada had written, "The Rainbow," engraved on it.

The Rainbow

Bow down in hope, in thanks, all ye who mourn;—

Where'in that peerless arche of radiant hues

Surpassing earthly tints,—the storm subdues!

Of nature's strife and tears 'tis heaven-born,

To soothe the sad, the sinning, and forlorn;

A lovely loving token to infuse

The hope, the faith, that pow'r divine endures

With latent good the woes by which we're torn.—

'Tis like a sweet repentance of the skies,

To beckon all by sense of sin opprest,—

Revealing harmony from tears and sighs!

A pledge:—that deep implanted in the breast

A hidden light may burn that never dies,

But bursts thro' clouds in purest hues exprest!

—A.A. Lovelace

Esther Eng
(1914–1970)

Esther Eng was a Chinese American and out lesbian filmmaker at a time when being either was difficult in its own right. She was born in San Francisco, California, on September 24, 1914, with the Chinese name Ng Kam-ha, to parents who had also been born in San Francisco. She was one of 10 children. Cantonese opera was popular at the time, and as a child, Esther was obsessed. As a teen, she worked at the box office at the Mandarin Theatre, which showcased Cantonese operas (including some with all-female casts), as well as tons of movies.

As China inched toward war with Japan, Esther's father formed a film production company with some friends to make a patriotic film and asked Esther, then 21, to coproduce it. "Heartaches" ("Sum Hun"), released in 1936, was shot in Hollywood in eight days—the first Cantonese-language film shot there. It starred Cantonese opera actress and Ng family friend Wai Kim-Fong. For the credits of the film, Esther changed her last name to Eng, which she thought American audiences would have an easier time pronouncing.

Esther and Wai took the film to Hong Kong, where it was so rapturously received that Esther decided to stay. At age 22, she directed her first film, *National Heroine* (1937), also starring Wai, about a woman pilot. The Hong Kong press loved writing about Esther—particularly her affairs with actresses and masculine manner of dress—and this attention fueled her career. She directed four more films in Hong Kong, notably the 1939 picture *It's a Women's World*, which had an all-female cast of 36. When the Second Sino-Japanese War escalated in October 1939, Esther returned to the United States. She made her best-known film, *Golden Gate Girl*, in 1941. The movie, which supported Chinese war efforts, featured a 3-month-old Bruce Lee in his first role (as a baby girl).

After the war and the passing of her father, Esther set up a film distribution company, Silver Light, to bring Cantonese-language films to the United States. She made three more films, then left the industry to open Bo Bo restaurant in New York City in 1950. She was 35. The restaurant was popular among Cantonese artists and performers, and she opened several more restaurants over the years. She worked on one final film in 1961, *Murder in New York Chinatown*, but she directed only exterior scenes. Esther died of cancer in 1970 at the age of 55. Although *Variety* and the *New York Times* wrote obituaries, her films have not survived and her career was largely forgotten until a 1995 article in *Variety*. In 2006, a box of her photos was fortuitously found in a San Francisco dumpster, which inspired the 2013 documentary *Golden Gate Silver Light*.

The Byron family continued to provide fodder for the press for decades. Lord Lovelace remarried in 1865 and died in 1893. Ada's son Byron eventually deserted the US Navy and died at age 26. Lady Byron passed away in 1860, and 10 years later, Harriet Beecher Stowe wrote a biography of her, titled *Lady Byron Vindicated.* Ada's younger son, Ralph, published a family biography in 1905 before passing away the following year. Her daughter, Lady Anne Blunt, was an artist and writer who, like her grandmother, married a poet.

> "I believe myself to possess a most singular combination of qualities exactly fitted to make me preeminently a discoverer of the hidden realities of nature."

No one ever built the Analytical Machine, but a complete Difference Engine was built in 2002 according to Babbage's plans—and it did exactly what it was supposed to.

As computer programming took off in the 1940s, Ada and Babbage's works were rediscovered. Alan Turing read Ada's notes and wrote about them. As more discussion and analysis of her work emerged, scholars debated Ada's authorship, with some claiming she'd taken credit for Babbage's work or overstated her contributions. Others have claimed that once it became apparent how important computer programming would be, the less believable it was that a woman could be a visionary in the field. In the late 1970s, the US Department of Defense named a software language Ada in her honor. Today, Ada Lovelace Day is celebrated every second Tuesday of October, dedicated to celebrating women in STEM.

MARY BLAIR

(1911–1978)

When riding on the "It's a Small World" ride at Disneyland, visitors may see a blonde girl holding a red balloon by the Eiffel Tower. The ride represents unity around the world, but this little girl is not French. She is the ride's American creator, Mary Blair, one of the most important Disney visionaries you've never heard of.

Mary Blair was born Mary Browne Robinson on October 21, 1911, in McAlester, Oklahoma, to John and Varda Robinson. She had a fraternal twin sister, Augusta, and an older sister, Margaret. The family moved to Texas before settling in Morgan Hill, California, in the San Francisco Bay Area. Mary was always creative and loved to paint. In high school, she won a national art contest and also participated in student government and the school newspaper. She was the valedictorian of her graduating class, and went on to attend San Jose State College, where she majored in fine art.

After a year at San Jose State, Mary transferred to the Chouinard Art Institute (now CalArts) in Los Angeles, where she had won a scholarship. She was a serious student and studied watercolor with renowned artist Pruett Carter. At Chouinard, she met and fell in love with another student, Lee Everett Blair. They were both extraordinarily talented: Lee had won an Olympic gold medal in the drawing and watercolors category at the 1932 Summer Olympics in Los Angeles (art was part of the Olympics until 1948). Mary and Lee graduated in 1933 and quickly married in the midst of the Great Depression. Around this time, Mary wrote to Lee: "We are artists dear, and in love with art and each other. We must make these loves coincide and melt into a beautiful, happy & rich life. That is our future and is real. We'll live to be happy and paint to express our happiness."

They continued their work after graduation, taking part in the famed California Watercolor Society, selling some paintings, and exhibiting their work in California and Texas, but they still had difficulty making ends meet. The couple lived in Los Angeles when animation was just taking off in Hollywood, and they got jobs in the burgeoning industry. Mary joined the Harman-Ising animation studio at Metro-Goldwyn-Mayer, and Lee eventually landed at Walt Disney Studios, where he worked as an animator on *Fantasia*. At Harman-Ising, Mary worked on Looney Tunes cartoons and was promoted to art director, but the male-dominated culture was toxic for her. Coworker Joe Barbera (later of Hanna-Barbera Productions) harassed her daily. She made it work for as long as she could, taking refuge in her own paintings on weekends, but after three years at Harman-Ising, she begged Lee to help her find a job at Disney.

In 1940, Mary was hired as a concept artist in Disney's Character Model Department, creating three-dimensional figures of characters to help the animators. Mary was amazed at the number of women in her new workplace—even her new boss was a woman. Walt Disney himself had gone out of his way to hire women, and the company had the highest percentage of female employees of all the Hollywood studios. After a few months, Mary was transferred to the story department, which better suited her talents. She worked on a proposed sequel to *Fantasia* that never got made, then began work on a story of a baby elephant, *Dumbo* (1941). Walt loved Mary's sketches of the mother and child elephants bonding through cage bars. Mary suffered several miscarriages and felt creatively stifled in her work at Disney, where the hours were long and weekend work was normal. She longed to get back to her own artwork, so, after only a little more than a year, she resigned.

Almost immediately after her departure, Walt decided to take a core group of his artists on a three-month trip to South America, part of a government-funded goodwill effort. Lee was among those invited. Mary had never left the country and was wildly jealous, so she boldly asked Walt if she could join. Walt agreed—and even hired her back. In fall 1941, the group of 18, which included Walt and Lillian Disney, set off for Rio de Janeiro, Brazil. Mary was the only female artist among them. The artists sketched and explored while Walt took meetings with dignitaries. One night, a worker called them for dinner by saying, "El Grupo Disney?" They loved the name, and it stuck. From then on, they were known as El Grupo. They went on to Buenos Aires, Argentina, followed by Bolivia, Peru, and Mexico. The trip transformed Mary's artistic style, as she replaced her usual muted tones with bright colors. Walt loved what he was seeing—which planted a seed of jealousy in Lee.

Because the South American trip was tied to two films financed by the US government, Mary had guaranteed employment with Disney when the group returned to the States. Walt named Mary art supervisor on the films *Saludos Amigos* (1942) and *The Three*

Caballeros (1944). Mary's was the only female name in the credits. Lee was drafted into the US Army in 1942, serving with the Art and Animation Unit in Washington, DC. While he was gone, Mary traveled to Mexico, Cuba, and the state of Georgia to create concept art for some new films. She relished the independence. Concept art entailed choosing a color palette for a film, designing characters, imagining scenes, and creating a style. It was the first step in the filmmaking process. From the concept art, storyboards were created and the script was written.

After Lee was discharged from the army in 1946, he decided to stay on the East Coast and form a company that created TV commercials, an emerging field. Mary followed him to Long Island, New York, but was able to keep her job at Disney. Because Walt loved Mary's work so much, he allowed her to work remotely. Mary began an actively bicoastal life, flying back and forth between New York to Los Angeles. Soon after the move East, at age 35, Mary found out she was pregnant. Her first son, Donovan, was born on February 12, 1947, while she was working on concept art for *Cinderella* (1950). The studio wanted *Cinderella* to be a low-budget production that would be a big hit at the box office. Mary used bright colors with basic lines to give the film a rich lushness on a budget, and also brought modernity into styling the costumes. Many of the film's iconic scenes came from Mary's concept art: the birds and mice helping Cinderella make a ballgown, the glass slipper left on the steps, the fairy godmother transforming a pumpkin into a carriage. When *Cinderella* was released, it was the hit the studio had hoped for.

"We are artists dear, and in love with art and each other. We must make these loves coincide and melt into a beautiful, happy & rich life. That is our future and is real. We'll live to be happy and paint to express our happiness."

Walt loved Mary's work so much that it was a source of great envy among the other artists at the studio, especially the male character animators who refused to veer from their typical methods into a new style. In their hands, Mary's modern graphic work often became traditional and rounded-off. A frequent refrain from Walt was, "Get Mary into this," a directive to bring her style back into the animation.

The next movie Mary worked on was *Alice in Wonderland* (1951). As the concept artist, her interpretation of the source material would influence the direction of the film, and she was responsible for creating the look of the film before there was even a script. Mary had just had her second son, Kevin, on August 15, 1950, and she spent the early months of his life at home in Long Island devising a whimsical, dreamy tone for the film: painting Alice falling upside down through the rabbit hole, Alice growing frighteningly giant compared to her surroundings, the Queen of Hearts calling her card minions. Walt loved Mary's work, but he was disappointed the film didn't do well at the box office. By that point, Mary had already moved on to her next project, *Peter Pan* (1953). She painted angelic mermaids in lagoons; the menacingly gray Skull Rock piercing the sky; and Peter, Wendy, John, and Michael flying past Big Ben. Walt was over the moon with the results and gave her the role of art director on the film.

In the midst of working on *Peter Pan*, Mary returned home early from a trip to the Disney Studios and discovered Lee with another woman. Life with Lee had grown more difficult over time. He did not share in the domestic labor of raising children or keeping a home, even though Mary had a full-time job that required a lot of travel. They had some hired help, but it wasn't enough. Worse still, Lee's frequent drinking had devolved into verbal—and sometimes physical—abuse. Mary felt divorce was not a socially acceptable option, and she did not tell anyone what was happening at home. She began drinking to cope. In 1953, she took drastic measures, quitting her job at Disney in the middle of working on *Sleeping Beauty* (1959) to focus on keeping her family together. Walt was disappointed, but he and Mary were such good friends that he stayed in touch, writing her letters and sending Christmas presents to her children.

In New York, Mary found a new freelance career as a designer and illustrator. For 10 years she worked on advertisements for brands like Johnson & Johnson, Nabisco, and Maxwell House Coffee. She designed sets for commercials and Radio City Music Hall and clothing for Lord & Taylor. She also illustrated children's books for the Simon & Schuster imprint Golden Books, including *I Can Fly* by Ruth Krauss. In 1963, Walt called Mary to ask if she would like to design a boat ride for the 1964 World's Fair. She jumped at the chance.

The theme was Peace Through Understanding, and the ride would be located in the United Nations Children's Pavilion, with ticket proceeds going to UNICEF. Walt visualized the ride as celebrating children of every culture in the world, calling it "It's a Small World." Mary had less than a year to design the ride and oversee its creation. Calling it the "most interesting job I've ever had," she immediately set to work designing cherubic children surrounded by graphic elements, bright colors, and iconic images typifying cultures around the world. The ride was Mary's art brought to life more fully than it had ever been. Built inside a Hollywood soundstage before being shipped to New York for the fair, it was a huge hit upon its arrival. At the end of the fair, Walt decided to install the ride at Disneyland, which had opened in 1955. Mary helped adapt it for its final home in Anaheim, California, with iterations later installed at Disney parks around the world.

Walt wanted to continue working with Mary, and she welcomed additional collaborations. He commissioned a ceramic mural inspired by "It's a Small World" for the new children's wing of the Jules Stein Eye Institute at UCLA, two huge murals for Tomorrowland at Disneyland, and a mural in one of the hotels at Walt Disney World, which was still under construction. Mary had barely started on these assignments when she received terrible news: Walt had lung cancer. He passed away only a few months later, on December 15, 1966. Mary didn't have a chance to say goodbye to her friend and champion. She honored him with her mural work, which took her through the end of the decade to complete.

Many of Cinderella's iconic scenes came from Mary's concept art: the birds and mice helping Cinderella make a ballgown, the glass slipper left on the steps, the fairy godmother transforming a pumpkin into a carriage.

After Mary finished the murals Walt had commissioned, no one at Disney would assign her more work. Historians have hypothesized that her colleagues still resented the favoritism Walt had shown her. Things were difficult at home: Lee's alcoholism was worse than ever, and Mary's oldest son, Donovan, was dealing with mental health issues. Doctors were at a loss as to how to help him, and Mary felt cornered into institutionalizing him. To pay the bills, Mary and Lee decided to sell their Long Island home and move back to Northern California.

Mary hoped that being closer to San Francisco and Los Angeles would help her continue her freelance illustration career, but no one would hire her. Lee's alcoholism resulted in multiple DUIs that led to a yearlong jail sentence. With her younger son in the navy, Mary was now alone. She began drinking more heavily. Lee got sober in jail, and after his release was longer abusive toward Mary, but it was too little too late. Mary Blair died of a cerebral hemorrhage on July 26, 1978, in Soquel, California, at the age of 66. Her death was barely mentioned in the press.

In the ensuing years, there has been a resurgence of support for Mary's artwork. In 1991, she was honored as a Disney Legend. Museum exhibitions of her work have been shown in New York, Tokyo, Los Angeles, and San Francisco. Many of today's Disney and Pixar filmmakers, like *Up* director Pete Docter, have been outspoken about Mary's influence on animation today. Her original artwork continues to set auction records, and several books on her work have been published, including a children's book about her life.

IDA B. WELLS

(1862–1931)

Ida B. Wells was born a slave in the midst of the Civil War. In her lifetime, she became a revolutionary anti-lynching activist, civil rights advocate, suffragist, and an influential journalist, all while raising four children.

Ida entered the world on July 16, 1862, the first child of two slaves: James (the son of an enslaved woman and her master) and Elizabeth Wells. The country was a year into the Civil War, and her birthplace of Holly Springs, Mississippi, was in the thick of the conflict.

Six months after Ida's birth, President Abraham Lincoln issued the Emancipation Proclamation, although slavery effectively ended only with the conclusion of the war and the ratification of the Thirteenth Amendment in December 1865. As a slave, Ida's father apprenticed to learn carpentry, and after emancipation, he was able to take a paying job with the carpenter for whom he had apprenticed. For the next five years, James had a stable paying position. In February 1870, the Fifteenth Amendment was ratified, giving black men the right to vote. James' employer wanted him to vote for the Democratic ticket, which promoted white supremacy. James refused and lost his job. Meanwhile, Ida's mother, Elizabeth, had been known as an outspoken slave who'd been consistently punished for her demeanor but persisted in speaking out. Elizabeth's skills as a cook reportedly saved her from worse punishment.

Ida grew up watching her parents take advantage of their growing powers under Reconstruction, and she also saw how their actions matched their beliefs. Her father was on the board of trustees for Rust College, which taught students of all ages and grades. Her parents stressed the importance of education, and Ida was an excellent student.

In 1878, when Ida was 16, a yellow fever epidemic hit Holly Springs hard. Both her parents died from the virus, as did one of her younger brothers. The eldest of her five remaining siblings, Ida was determined to keep her family together. She convinced a nearby school administrator she was 18, passed a teaching exam, and took a job at a local school to support her siblings. She finished her own education at night and on weekends.

After about three years, Ida and her sisters moved to Memphis, Tennessee, to live with their aunt, while her brothers apprenticed as carpenters. Ida became engaged in black society and continued teaching, commuting to a segregated public school 10 miles north in Woodstock, Tennessee.

On September 15, 1883, Ida was on a train heading to work in Woodstock. Two years earlier, Tennessee had been the first state to enact a railroad segregation statute in the United States. Before that time, slaves rode with their masters. Ida had purchased a first-class ticket. The first-class car was nonsmoking and reserved for whites. The other car could be rough, with the other passengers drinking and smoking. When the conductor collected the tickets, he told 21-year-old Ida she would have to leave the first-class car. She refused. He attempted to forcibly carry her to the other car, and she resisted by grabbing her seat and biting the conductor's arm. Two other white passengers helped the conductor drag Ida to the other car, ripping her dress in the process. Ida refused to change cars and instead got off the train. Through it all, she held on to her first-class ticket. She then sued the Chesapeake & Ohio Railroad—and initially won. She received a payment of $500 (about $13,000 in today's money) but the railroad appealed to the Tennessee Supreme Court, which sided with the railroad.

In her diary, Ida wrote of the loss: "I feel so disappointed because I had hoped such great things from my suit for my people generally. I have firmly believed all along that the law was on our side and would, when we appealed it, give us justice. I feel shorn of that belief and utterly discouraged, and just now if it were possible would gather my race in my arms and fly far away with them."

Ida saw the injustice both in the segregation on the train and in the law siding with that injustice. She turned to journalism to air her grievances, writing articles in black newspapers about race and politics under the name Iola while continuing to work as a teacher. Her contract was not renewed because of her criticism of segregated education, so she dedicated herself to journalism full time and bought an interest in the *Memphis Free Speech*, where she became an editor.

In March 1892, Ida's world was turned upside down when her friend Thomas Moss and two of his associates were lynched by a white mob. Moss, an integral member of the black community in Memphis, was a co-owner of the People's Grocery, a co-op market. Ida was godmother of Moss' daughter. Lynching had been on the rise throughout the 1880s, as whites felt threatened by the increasing rights, power, and economic well-being of the people they had once controlled. A University of Illinois study published in 1995 estimated that there was roughly one mob killing every week for *five decades* between 1880 and 1930. Ida refused to keep her mouth shut in response to injustice. For the next few months, she wrote a series of fiery articles condemning lynching and traveled around the country to study the terror more closely. She encouraged Memphis blacks to boycott streetcars, railways, and other white businesses, and even to leave the South (some estimates put the exodus at 6,000 people during the months Ida encouraged the idea). This call for boycott and civil disobedience later inspired civil rights leaders of the 1960s like Martin Luther King Jr. (who was also inspired by Mahatma Gandhi). Ida was in New York on May 27, 1892, three months after her friends were lynched, when one of her articles incited a mob to destroy the offices of the *Memphis Free Speech*. Because of the continued threats on her life, she never returned to Memphis.

Ida's research resulted in the pamphlet *Southern Horrors: Lynching in All Its Phases*, published in June 1892 (a month before she turned 30), which some scholars have cited as the beginning of investigative journalism. Frederick Douglass, then in his seventies, wrote Ida a letter that was published at the front of the pamphlet, stating, "You have dealt with the facts with cool, painstaking fidelity and left those naked and uncontradicted facts to speak for themselves." Ida proved with numbers that lynching was often motivated by economic jealousy, rather than the usual justification; the claim that a black man had raped a white woman. Ida found that in the instances of sexual contact between the victim and a white woman, it was typically consensual. She backed up this assertion with hard numbers.

Ida hit a raw nerve in Victorian America. The white press ripped into her, but she continued to write anti-lynching editorials for the

New York Age, a prominent black newspaper edited by T. Thomas Fortune, where she was a staff writer for the next few years. She embarked on two speaking tours of England and Ireland, attempting to sway international opinion on lynching. She knew that attracting international attention to the practice would make it a national issue, rather than a regional Southern one. She inspired the creation of many anti-lynching clubs while abroad, which the white American press hated, as they thought lynching in America was not the business of the British.

Frederick Douglass recruited Ida to cowrite a pamphlet with Ferdinand Lee Barnett, a Chicago lawyer and newspaper publisher, protesting the 1893 World's Fair in Chicago for excluding black participants. Ferdinand, a widower with two sons, was also a serious activist, and on June 27, 1895, after three postponements to accommodate Ida's speaking schedule, the two were married. Their wedding made the front page of the *New York Times*. Ida Wells-Barrett was one of the first women in the United States to hyphenate her married name. The Monday after her nuptials, she bought out *The Conservator*, Ferdinand's Chicago newspaper. She also published *A Red Record: Tabulated Statistics and Alleged Cause of Lynchings in the United States, 1892–1894*, which expanded on her research into lynching and was an early entrant in the field of data journalism. Ida aggregated newspaper accounts of lynchings that took place during the period, diving into the alleged crimes and specific incidents in which due process was denied. Using statistics, she showed how lynching was used as a strategy to encourage white supremacy, limit black rights, scare black people into submission, and promote a narrative among whites that black men were to be feared. She asserted that lynching was the white man's gambit to regain lost power.

Ida had her first son a year into her marriage. She had another son and two daughters over the next eight years, giving birth to her fourth child at age 42. During this time, Ida went into quasi-retirement, claiming motherhood was a job unto itself. Suffragist Susan B. Anthony complained, "Since you have gotten married, agitation seems practically to have ceased," but Ida still attended anti-lynching rallies and suffrage conventions (often bringing her children with her), and wrote editorials in *The Conservator*. In 1898, she was still nursing her son Herman when she traveled to Washington, DC, to lobby President William McKinley and Congress to establish a national anti-lynching law. (The fight would go on for 122 years; the Senate confirmed the first anti-lynching law in 2018.)

As Ida's children grew older, she had to consider the schooling options available to black children in Chicago. There was one integrated kindergarten, but the wait-list was long. So Ida decided to start one herself, located in the lecture room at Bethel Church, which served black community members and allowed them to use the space for free. It was the first kindergarten in the city created with black children in mind, although the school also accepted white children. Ida worked closely with Jane Addams of Hull House in Chicago to block the establishment of any legally segregated schools in Chicago.

In 1896, Ferdinand was appointed Illinois' first black assistant state attorney by the new state attorney, Charles Deneen, who went on to be the state's governor. Ferdinand was in the position for 14 years, and he argued in front of the Illinois Supreme Court many times, with great success.

The National Afro-American Council was an early civil rights organization in the United States led by Ida's former employer at the *New York Age*, T. Thomas Fortune, among others. Ida was the organization's secretary from its inception in 1898 until 1902. Booker T. Washington had risen to prominence in the 1890s, and his association with the National Afro-American Council was controversial. Many believed his approach was too conciliatory and accommodating, he was too willing to compromise black rights, and his expectations for black rights were too low. Ida was one of Washington's biggest critics. She was unfailingly blunt when she thought someone was compromising what she believed was right, and she wasn't always popular with the black elite because of her outspoken nature. She was left out of certain gatherings because some found her too controversial. Some scholars have cited Ida's blunt criticisms as a reason she has been left out of parts of civil rights history, while her contemporaries Booker T. Washington and W.E.B. Du Bois have been heralded. She was certainly more militant in her beliefs than many of her prominent male peers.

In August 1908, a race riot broke out in Springfield, Illinois, 200 miles south of Ida's home in Chicago. It lasted two days. Several thousand white citizens attacked the black community in Springfield, and the Illinois state militia had to be called. Two older black men were lynched. Homes were burned and stores were looted. The fact that this took place in Abraham Lincoln's home-town illustrated how far US race relations had sunk. Some white liberals teamed up with black civil rights advocates to prevent a recurrence. Six months later, on what would've been Lincoln's 100th birthday, the National Association for the Advancement of Colored People (NAACP) was born.

"You have dealt with the facts with cool, painstaking fidelity and left those naked and uncontradicted facts to speak for themselves."

—Frederick Douglass, in an 1892 letter to Ida B. Wells

At the NAACP's first gathering in February 1909, Ida gave a speech about her career fighting lynching, where she laid out what she'd learned ("Crimes against women is the excuse, not the cause") and described the best path forward, including the creation of a bureau of investigation that would publish details of lynching and nationalize the issue. As always, she used statistics to back up her claims. The meeting ended with a 40-person commit-tee being selected to govern the new group. Many, including Ida, thought she was a shoo-in, but when the list was announced, she wasn't included. W.E.B. Du Bois explained the political reasoning behind her absence from the list, then offered to add her name. Ida was insulted and refused the offer, but he added her name anyway. When the next NAACP meeting happened at the end of the year, Ida skipped it in favor of going to Cairo, Illinois, where a black man had been brutally lynched in front of a crowd of 10,000. She wanted to make sure a 1904 Illinois law requiring the removal of any sheriff whose prisoner was lynched was put into effect, and thanks to her efforts, it was. The press saw her as a singular hero, which likely didn't help her standing with the burgeoning NAACP. She maintained her membership, and even helped organize an April 1912 Chicago meeting with her husband. After that meeting, however, she began to officially lessen her involvement in the organization. Ida lost patience with what she saw as the group compromising its ideals. So she left the NAACP and focused her energy on all-black organizations, such as her own Negro Fellowship League, and on women's rights.

"Crimes against women is the excuse, not the cause."

Ida vilified gender discrimination as much as racial prejudice. During her trip to England in the 1890s, she had been inspired by the women's suffrage movement there and, concurrent with the National Afro-American Council, started the Ida B. Wells Club, the first club for black women in Chicago. On January 30, 1913, she founded what may have been the first suffrage club for black women, the Alpha Suffrage Club in Chicago. In addition to votes for women, one of its main goals was to organize women to ensure they elected candidates who would serve in the best interests of the black community. A few months later, in March, a suffrage march in Washington, DC, gathered together suffrage clubs from around the country the day before Woodrow Wilson was inaugurated as president of the United States. As leader of the Alpha Suffrage Club, Ida was invited. White suffragists, however, worried that the presence of black suffragists would offend Southern white suffragists and asked the black suffragists to march in the back of the parade. On the day of the parade, Ida stood on the sidelines until the white suffragists from Chicago passed by—then joined them. The rest of the Alpha Suffrage Club stayed at the back. Ida and the Alpha Suffrage Club worked hard in Chicago, and on June 25, 1913, women in Illinois gained the right to vote with the passage of the Illinois Equal Suffrage Act.

At the beginning of the 20th century, black Americans began to migrate from the South in great numbers. Lynching and lack of economic opportunity were both factors, and many arrived in Chicago. There wasn't always a place for the new residents to go, and the YMCA refused to house black men. (This changed as YMCA facilities for black men began to be built.) In 1910, Ida founded, funded, and served as president of the Negro Fellowship League, which had a rooming house for black men, placed black people in jobs, and served as a community center. To fund the Negro Fellowship League (Ida did not grow rich from publishing or from being well-known), she took a day job as the first black female probation officer in Chicago in 1913, serving for three years. There was a great need for the league, as the migration of black Americans increased following World War I—including approximately 250,000 people leaving Georgia alone between 1917 and 1924.

In 1930, at age 67, Ida ran for the Illinois State Senate as an independent. She was one of the first black women in the United States to run for public office. The election resulted in a crushing loss, as Ida came in third. She was disappointed that she didn't have more support from women voters.

The following year, in March 1931, Ida started feeling ill after a day of shopping. Two days later, she fell into a coma. On March 25, 1931, Ida died of kidney disease at age 68.

Three years before her death, Ida began work on her autobiography. She had already predicted she would be written out of history, and she had also seen others use her strategies without giving her credit. She knew if she did not record her story, no one else would. Although she didn't finish the book before she died, her daughter Alfreda Duster completed it on her behalf. *Crusade for Justice* was finally published in 1970. Some have cited Ida's acrimonious split with the NAACP as the reason she has not been better remembered, as the organization dominated the conversation around black rights and black history for decades. But Ida B. Wells worked not only for racial justice but also for gender equality. She challenged just about every existing power structure. The people in charge, the people who write history, were not motivated to remember someone who threatened them. But interest in Ida and her legacy continues to grow. The Chicago home in which Ida and her family lived from 1919 to 1929 is now a national historic landmark, and in February 2019, a major Chicago street was renamed Ida B. Wells Drive. In 2018, Ida's great-granddaughter raised $300,000 to build a monument honoring Ida in Chicago.

Madam C.J. Walker and Ida B. Wells

Madam C.J. Walker (page 99) and Ida B. Wells first met in 1906. It's unknown how their relationship progressed over the years, but by the September 1917 National Equal Rights Conference, they were close enough for Madam to take Ida to Irvington-on-Hudson, New York, and show her the in-progress Villa Lewaro. Ida recalled in her autobiography, "I asked her on one occasion what on earth she would do with a 30-room house. She said, 'I want plenty of room in which to entertain my friends. I have worked so hard all of my life that I would like to rest.'" Ida noted that she was impressed by how much success Madam had achieved in such a short time: "To see her phenomenal rise made me take pride anew in Negro womanhood." The next year, both Madam and Ida were furious when the exclusively male nominating committee for the National Race Congress for World Democracy chose only men to send to Paris for the peace talks at the end of World War I. They were a team who voiced their displeasure together.

Karen Sparck Jones
(1935–2007)

Every time you Google something, you have Karen
Sparck Jones to thank: All of today's search engines are
based on her research. Born on August 26, 1935, in Hud-
dersfield, England, Karen grew up during World War II
before attending Cambridge University, where she
studied history and philosophy. In her last year at Cambridge, Karen met Margaret Masterman, head of the new
Cambridge Language Research Unit (CLRU), which was
dedicated to the application of language to machines.
Karen graduated in 1956 and took a job as a teacher, but
in 1957, Masterman lured her back to Cambridge and she
began her doctoral studies in computer science. Karen
later said of Masterman: "She was a role model in that
she showed me there is nothing to stop women working
in this area."

At the CLRU, Karen met Roger Needham, who was
also working on his PhD. The two were married in 1958,
and together they built their own house, where they
lived for the next 40 years. Like Masterman, Karen kept
her maiden name. Karen and Roger chose not to have
children; instead, they focused on their careers.

In 1964, Karen earned her PhD and published her
thesis, "Synonymy and Semantic Classification," which
described how she programmed a machine with punch
cards containing the contents of *Roget's Thesaurus* to
make a computer understand that words could have
several meanings. Today, this study is still seen as one
of her greatest accomplishments. Eight years later, in
1972, she published a paper in the *Journal of Documen-
tation* that introduced the concept "term weighting," or
"inverse document frequency," which is the idea that
some words may be more important to a search than
others (for instance, using "the" as a search term will get

you nowhere). This paper became the foundation for the modern search engine in 1994 when Roger, a pioneer in cyber security, passed it to Mike Burrows, the founder of Alta Vista, one of the main search engines in the early days of the Internet. Today, nearly all search engines use the principles Karen laid out in her paper. She continued to research document retrieval for the rest of her career, in addition to teaching at Cambridge. However, despite her clear value to the university, Karen remained a lower-level contracted employee of the institution for decades. She was finally given a Readership, an academic rank in the United Kingdom, in 1994 and a full professorship in 1999—35 years after she completed her thesis. Karen later said, "Cambridge was in many ways not user-friendly, in the sense of women-friendly," and she worked to make both Cambridge and her field of computer science more welcoming to women. When she won the British Computer Society's Lovelace Medal in 2007, she said, "My slogan is: Computing is too important to be left to men." She retired three years after being made a professor to take care of Roger, who was sick with cancer; he passed away in March 2003. Karen was back to her research not long after, and she worked until her own death on April 4, 2007, also of cancer. She was 71. Today, Karen's work is recognized for being far ahead of its time. As a researcher, I am deeply grateful to her for making my work exponentially easier.

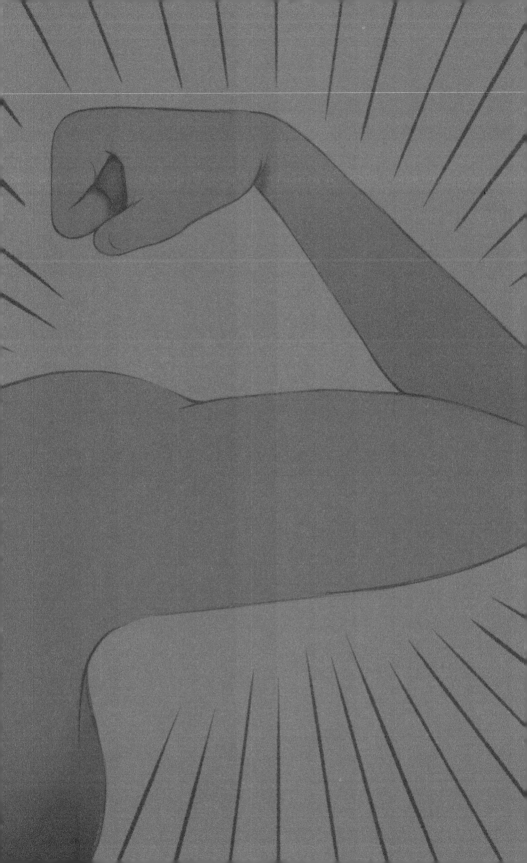

PART TWO

THE CHANGE-MAKERS

In 1884, early American politician and lawyer Belva Lockwood wrote, "We shall never have equal rights until we take them, nor equal respect until we command it." The courageous women in this section questioned the oppressive, racist, and sexist status quo. Their protests paved the way for institutional changes that have benefited women around the world.

MITSUYE ENDO

(1920–2006)

Far too few Americans know the history of the internment of Japanese-American citizens during World War II. Even fewer Americans know the story of Mitsuye Endo, a young woman from California who fought this injustice and refused to back down when pressured. Her actions helped right one of the most egregious wrongs in US history.

Mitsuye was born on May 10, 1920, in Sacramento, California. She was the second child of Japanese immigrants, Jinshiro and Shima Endo. Her father moved to the United States in 1916, returning to Japan to marry his wife. They came back to the United States together in 1918 and never returned to Japan, even to visit. The Endo family lived in the Japantown section of Sacramento, then one of the nation's largest and most tightly knit Japanese-American communities, with 3,400 residents and Japanese-owned grocery stores, theaters, churches, schools, and other businesses.

When Mitsuye graduated from high school, she attended secretarial school and got a job working for the state of California as a typist. This was considered a great job for a woman of Japanese descent, as discrimination against Japanese Americans, even in pre–World War II California, limited her options to working for the state or for a Japanese-owned business. Even state jobs were hard to land, especially for women.

On December 7, 1941, the Japanese military bombed Pearl Harbor. The US government had known there was a chance the country could be pulled into a war with Japan for some time—Mitsuye's brother had been drafted into the US Army earlier that year—and had been scouting out West Coast Japanese neighborhoods to identify "suspicious individuals" for more than a year. Immediately after Pearl Harbor, the FBI sprang into action. In the first day after the bombing, the FBI arrested about 1,300 "dangerous aliens." By the end of December, the FBI had arrested more than 3,000 people of Japanese descent, and the US Treasury froze the assets of anyone (including Mitsuye's parents) born in Japan.

In January, the state of California sent out a questionnaire to all its Japanese American employees, including Mitsuye, that asked whether they spoke Japanese, had attended a Japanese-language school, had ever visited Japan, belonged to any Japanese organizations, or subscribed to a Japanese-language newspaper. All the recipients of this questionnaire had been born in the United States, a requirement of their employment by the state.

President Franklin D. Roosevelt signed Executive Order 9066 on February 19, 1942, which established much of the West Coast as a military zone and authorized the removal of people of Japanese ancestry from these areas, out of fear (without evidence) that they might be loyal to Japan. The Japanese-American state employees who had received the questionnaire were advised not to come to work. Within a week, nearly 120,000 people of Japanese descent, most of whom were born in the United States, were ordered to vacate their homes. Mitsuye and her family were among them.

Some of Mitsuye's coworkers at the state of California were members of the Japanese American Citizens League (JACL was formed in 1929 to address issues of discrimination against the Japanese-American community). As a war with Japan loomed, the JACL went into overdrive trying to reassure the US government that the Japanese-American population were loyal US citizens. In January 1942, the president of the JACL, Saburo Kido, reached out to James C. Purcell, a lawyer with whom he had worked with in the past. Purcell was educated at Stanford Law School and had his own practice with a partner in San Francisco. Kido asked Purcell to put together a case that would challenge Japanese internment, and Purcell agreed to do so without taking a fee. He needed a model citizen who would be willing to dispute their detention through the court system.

In March 1942, President Roosevelt issued Executive Order 9102, which established the War Relocation Authority (WRA), which was responsible for speeding up the process of evacuation and internment. The WRA began building 10 relocation centers in remote inland areas throughout the United States to house evacuated Japanese Americans. In the meantime, people of Japanese ancestry were directed to assembly centers near their homes, where the US military assembled and trans-ported the evacuees. Mitsuye and her family were evacuated to the Walerga Assembly Center near Sacramento, where they remained for about a month. They were then moved to Tule Lake Segregation Center, near the California–Oregon border in Modoc County, California.

In April 1942, Mitsuye and all her American coworkers were officially fired from their jobs. The state of California was explicit that the firing was because of their ancestry, and essentially accused them of being Japanese citizens who were disloyal to the United States. In the first few months that Mitsuye was at Tule Lake, representatives for Purcell contacted about 100 former state of California employees, seeking an ideal candidate for Purcell to represent. Purcell chose Mitsuye Endo.

Mitsuye was the ideal plaintiff because she had never been to Japan, was Protestant (not Buddhist), did not attend a Japanese school, and didn't read or speak Japanese. Moreover, her parents didn't subscribe to a Japanese-language newspaper, and her brother was in the army. On paper, Mitsuye represented the ideal loyal American, impossible for the courts to fault. Purcell wrote to her—they never met in person—and convinced her to allow him to file a habeas corpus petition, which forces the court to determine whether a person's imprisonment is lawful, on her behalf. To say Mitsuye was hesitant to be the face of this case would be an understatement. In the only interview she ever gave, to author John Tateishi for his 2012 book *And Justice for All*, she shared, "When they came and asked me about it, I said, well, can't you have someone else do it first. It was awfully hard for me. I agreed to do it at that moment, because they said it's for the good of everybody, and so I said, well if that's it, I'll go ahead and do it."

Meanwhile, the American Civil Liberties Union (ACLU) was looking for a test case to challenge internment. They discovered Purcell's intention to file a habeas corpus petition on behalf of Mitsuye, and at first they hoped to take over the case. Instead, the ACLU signed onto the case as *amicus curiae*, or friend of the court, which meant they could submit a brief with the intention of influencing the court's decision. Purcell filed the habeas corpus against Milton Eisenhower, head of the WRA (and brother of the future president), with the federal district in San Francisco on July 13, 1942. Just a week later, on July 20, Judge Michael Roche asked for arguments to proceed immediately. The quick turnaround shocked both Purcell and the lawyer for the government, Deputy US Attorney Alfonso J. Zirpoli. They thought the purpose of that hearing was to set a time for an argument, not for the actual argument itself. Purcell later told author and historian Peter Irons, "He tried to catch me unprepared. Fortunately I had done my homework."

Purcell argued in front of Judge Roche that the internment was a form of undeclared martial law, given that a previous Supreme Court opinion had ruled that martial law can't exist while courts are open. A habeas corpus petition is supposed to speed things up and make judges rule more quickly. Judge Roche announced he would make his decision in 15 days' time.

That didn't happen. Instead, Judge Roche purposely failed to issue a decision for nearly a year. That's a whole year that Mitsuye remained in detention at Tule Lake Relocation Center, which consisted of poorly built, identical barracks surrounded by barbed wire fences and tall guard towers. Residents struggled to maintain their identity. Elevation was at 4,000 feet, making for long, cold winters and hot, dry summers. At times, there was not enough food. But the judge did not say a word.

It wasn't until the Supreme Court issued decisions in two related cases the following summer that Judge Roche finally made a call in Mitsuye's case. In the first few days of July 1943, he dismissed Mitsuye's petition. In just two sentences, Judge Roche said Mitsuye had not exhausted her options for attempting to leave Tule Lake. This was absolutely false. When her habeas corpus petition was first filed, there was no path available for detained Japanese Americans to leave the internment camps. Mitsuye had applied for leave clearance once the option became available seven months later—after the habeas corpus was filed but before the ruling. It was the only administrative opportunity the WRA made available. The WRA hadn't yet made a decision regarding her leave application, but it didn't matter. It didn't affect the ruling.

A month after the judge dismissed Mitsuye's case, the WRA granted Mitsuye's application for leave. The top lawyer for the WRA, Philip Glick, met with Mitsuye at Tule Lake. He encouraged her to take the opportunity to leave the camp. Years later, he recalled telling her, "Miss Endo, you're clearly a person who has been loyal to the United States all the time. . . . All you need do is ask for the right to leave the center and you can go. Any leave we grant you will expressly exclude return to the restricted area, but we'll help you relocate anywhere else in the United States." This was a strategy to prevent Mitsuye from pursuing the case and filing an appeal. In exchange, however, Mitsuye would not be able to return home to Sacramento or to her job for the state of California. The military zone along the West Coast was still in effect, and Japanese Americans were not allowed there. The offer was tempting. Some of Mitsuye's friends and extended family had been granted leave. She was likely intimidated, as Glick was powerful and held her freedom in his hands. Life outside the internment camp would be much easier, but if she took this deal, the case would be dropped. She later explained her decision to stay in the camps: "I wanted to prove that we of Japanese ancestry were not guilty of any crime and that we were loyal American citizens."

A few days later, Mitsuye's lawyer filed an appeal with the US Court of Appeals for the Ninth Circuit on her behalf. Behind the scenes, the ACLU was debating whether they should continue to support the Endo case. They even told Purcell to encourage Mitsuye to take the WRA's offer. They were focused on raising the constitutionality of detention in front of the Supreme Court as soon as possible, and they had a potential case with the plaintiff Fred Korematsu. He had evaded the order to evacuate California, even undergoing plastic surgery in an attempt to remain in hiding. His case directly challenged the constitutionality of Executive Order 9066.

Soon after Purcell filed Mitsuye's appeal, the WRA transferred Mitsuye and her family to a new internment camp, the Topaz War Relocation Center, about 140 miles southwest of Salt Lake City in the Sevier Desert. The camp had cold, harsh winters with temperatures often near 0 degrees Fahrenheit, and searingly hot summers at 90 degrees Fahrenheit or higher—a tough adjustment for Bay Area residents used to milder weather. Four or five families squeezed into a single barrack, and there were meager food rations. Various jobs were available to Topaz residents, and Mitsuye earned about $14 a month working as a secretary. Fred Korematsu was also interned at Topaz.

Mitsuye's move coincided with another loyalty questionnaire and a resulting shuffle among internment camps to isolate disloyals in a single location. The government hoped transferring Mitsuye would cause her to stop the appeal and give up her case. This action also jeopardized the future of her case because it moved her out of the district of the Court of Appeals in San Francisco. The court could now decide her case was no longer in its jurisdiction, rule on the case, or certify her case, making it eligible to be argued in the Supreme Court. When the Supreme Court agreed to certify the case in May 1944, it ordered both the Endo and Korematsu cases to be argued when the next term started in October.

"I agreed to do it at that moment, because they said it's for the good of everybody, and so I said, well if that's it, I'll go ahead and do it."

But that meant at least six more months at Topaz for Mitsuye.

Mitsuye said of the ordeal, "During that time in camp, I was anxious to have my case settled because most of my friends had already gone out, been relocated, and I was anxious to get out too. But I was told to remain there until I got a notice from our attorney that I could leave."

Purcell argued Mitsuye's case in front of the Supreme Court on October 12, 1944. Mitsuye never appeared in court, at any level of the case, and that day she was at work in her job as a secretary at Topaz. Purcell cited past Supreme Court decisions in habeas corpus cases to argue that because of the right to due process (a trial) guaranteed to citizens by the Fifth Amendment to the US Constitution, the military did not have the power to imprison a person without trial when they hadn't been charged for a crime and martial law had not been declared. The amicus briefs filed by the ACLU supported that argument and added that even if Congress had allowed a suspension of rights under martial law, that authorization would have been invalid because there had not been an invasion or rebellion on the mainland of the United States or other justifiable cause.

On December 18, 1944, the Supreme Court ruled unanimously in Mitsuye's favor. Justice William O. Douglas wrote the Court's opinion, declining to address the underlying constitutional issues but noting that Mitsuye and other loyal citizens should be released from relocation centers. The justices did not go so far as to call the detention unconstitutional, although Justice Frank Murphy wrote a concurring opinion in which he called it "racial discrimination."

The day before the ruling, however, Public Proclamation No. 21 declared that all Japanese-American evacuees were free to return to their homes starting on January 2, 1945 (although it would take the rest of the year for the last of them to leave the internment camps). At the time, 85,000 Japanese Americans were still detained. Interesting timing, right?

Internally, there was discussion among the Supreme Court justices about why the Endo decision took so long to come out. They had settled the case on October 16, just four days after arguments were heard. Justice Douglas finished his 24-page opinion and sent it to his colleagues on November 8. Later that month, on November 28, Justice Douglas sent a memorandum to Chief Justice Harlan Stone, writing, "Endo . . . is a citizen, insisting on her right to be released—a right which we all agree she has. I feel strongly that we should act promptly and not lend our aid in compounding the wrong through our inaction any longer than necessary to reach a decision." It's rumored that the Chief Justice held the decision for political reasons. President Roosevelt was elected to his fourth term in office on November 7, 1944. When a date was finally settled to release the decision, 41 days later, two justices reportedly warned the government so they could prepare their response.

The Supreme Court announced its decision in the Korematsu case the same day it ruled on Mitsuye, upholding the evacuation of Japanese Americans as legal, even though its ruling on Mitsuye was that the actual *detention* was illegal. Of the four cases addressing internment that went before the Supreme Court, only Mitsuye's was successful.

Mitsuye spent more than three years in detention by the US government. She was instrumental in restoring the freedom of nearly 100,000 Japanese Americans, but she was also very publicly scrutinized. She later shared, "I was very young, and I was very shy, so it was awfully hard to have this thing happen to me."

Mitsuye met Kenneth Tsutsumi at the Topaz War Relocation Center, and they moved to Chicago when Mitsuye was offered a job as an office manager with the mayor of Chicago's committee on human relations. The couple was married a year later, on November 22, 1946. Mitsuye took Kenneth's last name, which helped distance her from the case. She and Kenneth had three children, two daughters and a son, and raised them in a close-knit Japanese American community. After internment ended, many Japanese Americans moved to the Midwest and East Coast instead of returning West. Mitsuye rarely spoke about her time in internment, and her daughter, Terry, told the *Chicago Tribune* she hadn't known about her mother's role in the Supreme Court case until she was in her twenties. In 1982, California Governor Jerry Brown gave $5,000 as symbolic compensation to all the Japanese American state employees who were dismissed following Pearl Harbor. Kenneth passed away in 1988, and Mitsuye moved in with her daughter in the Chicago suburbs. She was a grandmother to eight.

Mitsuye Tsutsumi, née Endo, passed away on April 14, 2006, in a Willowbrook, Illinois, nursing home after a battle with cancer. She was 85 years old.

Looking back decades later, Mitsuye was self-deprecating: "Actually I didn't do too much. It was all my attorney's effort." But the case could have disappeared at any second with only a word from Mitsuye. And yet, when offered freedom and the ability to move on with her life, she voluntarily remained locked up. She had no idea what the outcome would be. In fact, she told Tateishi, "I never imagined it would go to the Supreme Court. In fact, I thought it might be thrown out of court because of all that bad sentiment toward [Japanese Americans]." She chose to live with that uncertainty for years so tens of thousands of strangers in the same position would have a chance at freedom.

POLICARPA SALAVARRIETA

(c. 1795–1817)

Policarpa Salavarrieta lived in a time of upheaval, when the people of present-day Colombia were in the midst of rebellion and bucking the tyrannical rule of the Spanish empire. She played an active role in the revolution, inspired a nation, and became a legend.

Policarpa was born around 1795 in the town of Guaduas, in what was then the Spanish viceroyalty of New Grenada, and is now modern-day Colombia. It's possible her parents named her Gregoria Hipolita or Gregoria Apolinaria, and Policarpa was a nickname. She went by Policarpa before she later (perhaps posthumously) was given the moniker La Pola. Guaduas, about 70 miles northwest of present-day Bogotá, was a small tropical town with a river running through its center. Policarpa likely had a large, close family, native but descended from Spaniards, an ethnicity that was referred to as Creole. Her parents died when she was young, perhaps about 7 years old, and Policarpa began working as a seamstress.

The town where Policarpa grew up had been involved in revolutionary movements against the Spanish colonial government several decades before Policarpa's birth, and she was raised in an atmosphere of lingering rebellious sentiment. Guaduas was on the route from the Caribbean to the capital in Bogotá, and people passed through and spread the news and opinions of the day. When Policarpa was about 13, the Spanish colonies were plunged into a state of uncertainty when Napoleon attacked Spain and took King Ferdinand VII and the royal family captive. In 1808, Napoleon made his brother Joseph the nominal king of Spain in what was really an extension of his own empire. The Spanish people didn't take the imposition quietly. They set up their own governing junta, promising to rule in Ferdinand VII's name until he was freed. When the news of Ferdinand VII's capture reached the colonies in the Americas, some cities took the opportunity to create their own juntas. Royalist viceroys—the Spanish government's authorities in the Americas—stamped out many of these attempts, but a seed was planted.

Dr. Camilo Torres wrote a *memorial de agravios*, or memorial of grievances, in November 1809 with the intention of sending it to the governing junta in Spain. The memorial contained specific complaints about the viceroyalties and a general overarching question of whether Spain had the right to rule the Americas, a more populous, larger geographical area. Before the *memorial de agravios* could be sent, the situation in Spain deteriorated even further, with Napoleon seizing control of the Spanish cities and juntas. This weakened the opposition of Spanish viceroys in the Americas and strengthened the resolve of the American juntas.

On July 20, 1810, when Policarpa was around 15 years old, a junta was created in Bogotá, the capital of the viceroyalty of New Grenada and the closest city to Policarpa's home. The junta was still nominally loyal to Ferdinand VII, but gave itself the authority to lead in his stead. Gradually, many of the juntas in what is now Colombia joined together into a loose federation, called the United Provinces of New Grenada, led by Dr. Torres. But the junta in Bogotá created its own federation, called Cundinamarca. The next few years were tumultuous, with power changing hands among the juntas, and the royalists vying for control.

Policarpa began participating in the revolution. She was known to be smart and outspoken, and she strongly believed in the cause of independence. Her brothers were involved in the movement, likely as guerillas. It was common for women to participate in the cause by pushing men into service, but Policarpa took a more active role. She passed along information she heard from visitors in Guaduas to the rebels and acted as a courier between different rebel groups.

Soon, possibly to escape royalists in her hometown who had caught on to her political activities, Policarpa moved to Bogotá, where she was unknown. She brought letters of recommendation from guerilla leaders in the Guaduas area for Andrea Ricaurte de Lozano, a revolutionary leader in Bogotá who hosted a network of women spies in her home. Andrea agreed to let Policarpa stay and to integrate her into the spy network. Policarpa began working as a seamstress in the homes of wealthy royalist women, where she quietly sewed and picked up important information to share with patriots. She also swiped useful documents, and passed messages between rebel groups, and possibly supplied guns. She visited guerillas in prison and carried messages, and she encouraged men who'd been drafted into the royalist army to abandon their posts and join the rebel cause. According to some accounts, she sewed uniforms for the guerilla forces while working in royalist homes.

The home of Andrea Ricaurte de Lozano was a general meeting place for Bogotán rebels, and there Policarpa met Alejo Sabarain, who was also involved in the rebel movement. They fell deeply in love and shared a great passion for the cause of independence.

Andrea later said of Policarpa's involvement with the revolutionary movement: "With the arrival of Policarpa the political work accelerated, and as she was unknown in the city, she came and went with liberty, facilitating correspondence with the juntas and the guerrillas." Some historians believe Policarpa participated in battles, although this is unconfirmed. Her contributions to the rebel cause, however, are undeniable.

Ferdinand VII returned to the Spanish throne in 1814, and he quickly reasserted his control over the Americas. In 1815 (quickly, by 19th-century standards), General Pablo Morillo and his army of 5,000 to 10,000 veteran soldiers landed at Cartagena. The city was under siege for more than three months before it fell, and Morillo and his army marched into the interior toward Bogotá. In May 1816, Morilla's forces officially retook Bogotá. Morilla set up a military court to make an example of the crown's enemies. His presence raised the stakes for the rebels, and a reign of terror ensued. Hundreds of men and women were imprisoned. Some were expelled from the country and others were executed.

In fall 1817, Policarpa's love, Alejo, was captured by the royalists and found to be carrying documents that detailed revolutionary actions. It's possible that the documents related to rebel leaders' escape from jail. The documents named Policarpa as part of the movement. A warrant was issued for her arrest.

As royalist soldiers approached Andrea's home, Policarpa and her colleagues rushed to burn papers documenting rebel movements and naming participants. Because Policarpa was apprehended in a woman's space—the kitchen—the soldiers did not think to check the fires or suspect the women tending to them. Policarpa was able to save much of the integrity of the rebel movement. When the soldiers questioned Andrea, she denied any involvement or knowledge of Policarpa's activites. Even though they'd just arrested a woman, the soldiers never suspected they had hit upon a whole network of spies, and the womens' work continued.

Policarpa was held at the Colegio del Rosario, where Morillo's troops had converted the classrooms into a prison. In early

November 1817, she was put on trial before the Council of War and found guilty of espionage and treason. She was sentenced to death, along with several others, although reports vary on the number of people charged. It's likely that Alejo was slated to be executed alongside her.

> "Although I am young and a woman, I have enough courage to suffer this death and a thousand more deaths. Do not forget this example."

At sunrise on November 14, 1817, Policarpa, Alejo, and their fellow condemned prisoners were marched into the Plaza Mayor in the center of Bogotá. According to legend (and this is really where the legends pick up steam), Policarpa received permission to wear her own clothes, a skirt and a shawl, to the execution. In front of a firing squad, She refused to cover her eyes, kneel, or turn her back to the riflemen. Instead, she shouted to the crowd, "Indolent people! How different your fate would be if you knew the price of freedom! But it is not too late. See that although I am young and a woman, I have enough courage to suffer this death and a thousand more deaths. Do not forget this example."

And with that, the firing squad killed Policarpa and her compatriots. Policarpa was just 21 years old.

As part of the vicious campaign waged by General Morillo, more than 300 men and women were executed between 1815 and 1819. But Policarpa's death in particular sparked outrage among the people and inspired many to join the fight for independence and turn against the Spanish government. Policarpa became a national hero, a martyr, and a symbol of patriotism. Her story quickly passed into folklore and was told through plays, poems, songs, and prose, even before the Spanish were finally driven from New Grenada in 1823.

Today, Colombia celebrates Women's Day each year on November 14, the anniversary of Policarpa's death. She is considered the most recognized woman in Colombia's history.

A neighborhood in Bogotá carries her full name, and there are many schools and stores named after her. There are statues of Policarpa in Bogotá, Guaduas, and other locations in Colombia. In 1910, as part of Colombia's celebration of 100 years of independence (the date is celebrated from the creation of the junta in Bogotá), a postage stamp with Policarpa's portrait was released, making her the first Latin American woman to be celebrated on a stamp. Another tribute during the 1910 celebration was the release of *Pola* beer, which featured her visage on the label. To this day, the word *pola* is often used in Colombia to refer to beer. In 1995, Policarpa was placed on the 10,000-peso bill in Colombia. Aside from an allegorical figure, she is the only woman to be featured on Colombian currency. On the back of the bill is an image of her hometown, Guaduas.

More than two centuries later, Policarpa Salavarrieta's courage, dedication, and patriotism continue to inspire the people of Colombia.

THE TRUNG SISTERS

(c. 14–43 CE)

In the first century CE, nearly a century into Chinese occupation, two sisters from what is now Northern Vietnam started the first rebellion against their overlords and won. Although the success of the campaign was short-lived, their resistance and courage became a shining beacon of inspiration—for both men and women—over the next 2,000 years of Vietnamese history.

Trung Trac and her younger sister, Trung Nhi, were born in the village of Me Linh, northeast of what's now the capital city of Hanoi, around 14 CE. Their father served as the Lac lord, or ruling landed aristocracy, for the area. The sisters were descended from the Hung kings of the earliest proto-Vietnamese state, who themselves were said to descend from "a union between a dragon and a fairy," possibly through their mother's side (although because the principal capital of the Hung Kingdom was the Trung sisters' hometown of Me Linh, it could have been through their father's side). The Trung family ruled over the village. As is common with nobility in any society, the sisters were taught to value patriotism, bravery, and virtue, and they likely were trained in the ways of war. They were also raised to be strong and independent.

It may come as a surprise to learn that, so early in history, the sisters were raised to be strong and independent. In fact, their native society was matrilineal, but Chinese invaders brought the patriarchy of Confucianism to the area. The Han empire of China conquered the region in 111 BCE, and for many years, there was a loose understanding with the Lac lords enabling them to retain power in their districts. But around 35 CE, a new Chinese governor, To Dinh, began to alter that policy. He instituted laws to assimilate the area to the culture of the Han dynasty and changed the matrilineal laws regarding land inheritance so property would be passed down through sons. He also raised taxes, demanded bribes, and took control from the Lac lords.

At the same time, elder sister Trung Trac married Thi Sach, the son of a neighboring Lac lord from the Chu Dien province. Trung Trac and Thi Sach were enraged by To Dinh's changes and sought to mobilize the other Lac lords against him. It's unclear whether To Dinh knew the extent of Trung Trac's involvement—or whether she was actually involved. Nevertheless, Thi Sach was arrested and Trung Trac was not. In 39 CE, To Dinh ordered Thi Sach's execution, and he was killed.

Instead of donning traditional mourning clothes, Trung Trac wore armor. She vowed to take revenge and to continue the mission for which her husband had died. Her first order of business was declaring war against the Chinese. She and Trung Nhi led the rebellion, both figuratively and literally—they picked up swords and were at the front of the insurgency. A legend tells of Trung Trac announcing to her troops her goals of taking back the country, avenging her husband's death, and restoring the Hung Kings' lineage.

The Trung sisters' army purportedly comprised 80,000 men and women, both peasants and aristocracy, who welcomed the opportunity to throw off their overlords. Trung Trac and Trung Nhi rode elephants into battle. Their army had many women generals, and some say more than half were women. One may have been the sisters' mother. Another general, Phung Thi Chinh, was reportedly heavily pregnant and gave birth in the thick of battle. She then strapped her newborn baby to her back and continued the fight.

Trung Trac, Trung Nhi, and their armies quickly moved through the land, taking back control from the Han Chinese. Trung Nhi in particular was an exceptional warrior, and the army was renowned for its acts of valor. The armies came for governor To Dinh, but he escaped in the nick of time. Some sources claim he was able to get past the army because he disguised himself by shaving his head and beard. But once back in China, To Dinh was either arrested or exiled on orders of his boss, the Han emperor.

The Trung sisters and their army took back control of 65 citadels from the Han. It was the first uprising against the Chinese in the approximately 150 years they'd been occupying what is now Vietnam. In 40 CE, the Trung sisters declared themselves joint queens of Vietnam, although some sources claim only Trung Trac was made queen. The sisters made their hometown of Me Linh the capital of the new kingdom, and they immediately abolished To Dinh's taxes. They restored laws to what they had been before Chinese rule, including returning inheritances to the maternal line. They were beloved, popular leaders.

But the Chinese emperor wasn't about to let go of this profitable territory without another fight. Although Trung Trac and Trung Nhi had restored dignity to their homeland, the emperor was making plans to conquer Vietnam again. In 42 CE, after two years of the Trung sisters' rule, the emperor sent one of his best generals, Ma Yuan, to attack the territory. This was a much tougher fight for the sisters. Ma Yuan, a skilled strategist, descended upon Vietnam with

20,000 of his best, most experienced soldiers. His army was ruthless and initially met with little resistance. The Trung sisters' army was comparatively untrained and lacked adequate supplies.

Trung Trac and Trung Nhi had clash after clash with Ma Yuan, including a major one near present-day Hanoi. Many supporters abandoned the cause as the fighting intensified and the Chinese armies gained reinforcements. In 43 CE, the sisters eventually retreated to defend their hometown of Me Linh. When it appeared there was no way to win, the Trung sisters drowned themselves in the River Day, near where it connects to the Red River, instead of surrendering to Chinese rule.

Instead of donning traditional mourning clothes, Trung Trac wore armor. She vowed to take revenge and to continue the mission for which her husband had died.

While this is the popularly accepted story of the sisters' deaths, it is also written that Ma Yuan captured and killed the sisters, then sent their heads to the emperor in China; other accounts say the sisters ascended to heaven.

According to legend, Ma Yuan had the Trung sisters' bronze war drums melted down to make pillars marking the southern border of the Chinese empire. Although the locations of these pillars were marked on maps throughout the years, their existence has never been confirmed.

The war went on after the deaths of Trung Trac and Trung Nhi, and thousands of soldiers were killed. Finally, the people of Vietnam fell back under Chinese control. Most of the Lac lords submitted to Chinese rule; those who didn't were killed. Ma Yuan immediately revised the laws so they were in line with Chinese policy, which more forcefully assimilated the Vietnamese people into Chinese culture. Vietnam was under Chinese control for the next 900 years, until 939 CE.

However, the Trung sisters' efforts and triumphs gave the Vietnamese people a legacy and story to hold on to. They became collectively known as Hai Ba Trung (Two Ladies Trung), and even though they ultimately failed in their mission, they were seen as symbols of resistance to foreign occupation, which is central to the Vietnamese culture and national identity. When Vietnam was later under French control, the Trung sisters once again became symbols of freedom, hope, patriotism, and resistance.

The sisters also set a precedent for the role of women in the fight against oppression. Another infamous rebellion against the Chinese took place in 248 CE, and it was also led by a woman, Ba Trieu. In the 19th and 20th centuries, Vietnamese women fought alongside Vietnamese men against the French, and were also crucial in fighting the American army during the Vietnam War.

In the nearly 2,000 years that have passed since Hai Ba Trung lived, countless people have told their story in countless different ways. A 13th-century historian, Le Van Huu, lamented, "What a pity that, for a thousand years after this, the men of our land bowed their heads, folded their arms, and served the northerners; how shameful this is in comparison with the two Trung sisters, who were women! Ah, it is enough to make one want to die!"

Because the sisters lived so long ago, and were often written about as near-deities, a popular cult has formed around them. About 200 temples are dedicated to the Trung sisters, and the two biggest are in Hanoi and their hometown of Me Linh. The Hanoi temple is known as Den Hai Ba Trung (Two Ladies Trung Temple). During a drought around 1142 CE, King Ly Anh Tong allegedly went to the Trung sisters' ancestral temple in Me Linh and ordered the Buddhist monks there to pray for rain. It rained, and the air was refreshed. The king was pleased. That night, he dreamed of two beautiful women wearing green robes over red trousers, with red hats and red sashes, riding steel horses. They said they were the Trung sisters and had brought the rain from heaven above. When the king woke up, he ordered the temple to be restored and established rituals for offering the sisters a ceremonial sacrifice. They appeared again in the king's dream and asked that another temple be built for them at the location where Den Hai Ba Trung now stands. Since then, the sisters have been known to help in times of flood or drought.

Another legend surrounds the statues of the sisters at Den Hai Ba Trung. It's said that when the sisters threw themselves in the River Day, they turned into stone and floated downstream, possibly standing guard and beaming light to scare away invading enemy boats. Today, schools, hospitals, and streets throughout Vietnam carry the Trung sisters' names. Songs and plays have been written about them, and their story is taught in schools. Every year, in the second lunar month, a major festival at Den Hai Ba Trung celebrates their feats. As part of the festival, the statues of Trung Trac and Trung Nhi are bathed in water from the nearby Red River.

Two millennia later, the courage and strength of Trung Trac and Trung Nhi are still celebrated. Their impact on Vietnamese culture and the future of their people is unparalleled.

Patsy Takemoto Mink
(1927–2002)

Patsy Takemoto Mink was the first woman of color elected to the US Congress, and she used her power to advocate for other women. She was born on December 6, 1927, in Paia on the island of Maui in the territory of Hawaii. Her grandparents came to Hawaii from Japan to work in the sugarcane fields, and her father was a civil engineer who surveyed land for the local sugar plantation. Although Patsy's family was middle class when she was growing up, she saw economic inequality up close on the plantation. The Pearl Harbor attacks took place the day after her fourteenth birthday, and soon afterward her father was taken away for a night and questioned, which terrified her and made civil rights an issue close to her heart.

Patsy was the valedictorian and the first woman class president when she graduated from Maui High School in 1944. She had always wanted to become a doctor and graduated with degrees in zoology and chemistry from the University of Hawaii in 1948, but although she applied to dozens of medical schools, they all rejected her—likely because of her race and gender. She chose law school as a backup and was one of just two women in her class at the University of Chicago. There she met a geology graduate student named John Francis Mink. They married within months and had a daughter, Gwendolyn, not long after.

Patsy soon found that none of the Chicago law firms would hire a woman, so she and her small family moved back to Hawaii. Patsy became the first Japanese-American woman admitted to the Hawaii bar in 1953, but Hawaiian firms also closed their doors to her. So she opened up her own practice and taught at the University of Hawaii.

Patsy soon became involved in politics. She founded the Oahu Young Democrats in 1954, worked as an attorney for the Hawaii Territorial Legislature in 1955, and was elected to that legislature in 1956 (the first Japanese-American woman to serve) and to the Hawaii Senate in 1958. Hawaii became a state in 1959, and Patsy gained attention by giving a speech at the Democratic National Convention in 1960. In 1964, when a second US House seat was created for Hawaii, Patsy ran for Congress and won. She was the first Asian-American woman and the first woman of color elected to Congress, and she arrived just in time to voice her support for the civil rights movement.

Patsy worked extensively on education issues, vocally opposed the Vietnam War (even independently meeting with North Vietnamese officials for peace talks in Paris), and did her best to represent the interests of her dual constituents: women and Hawaii. She notably opposed the Supreme Court nomination of George Carswell, which led to Harry Blackmun's appointment (he would go on to write the *Roe v. Wade* decision). In 1972, she coauthored Title IX, legislation that outlawed sexual discrimination in institutions receiving federal funding. This bill became known for its effect on women's sports, but it also increased women's representation at universities and in the workforce. That same year, Patsy had a brief, symbolic campaign for president.

In 1976, after more than a decade in Congress, she decided to run for US Senate. She lost, but remained involved in politics, serving as assistant secretary of state for Oceans and International Environmental and Scientific Affairs in President Jimmy Carter's administration, spending four years on the Honolulu City Council, and making failed runs for governor of Hawaii and mayor of Honolulu. In 1990, after 14 years away, she ran for her old Congressional seat and won. The social welfare legislation she'd worked on her first time in Congress was under attack, and she worked to protect it.

On September 28, 2002, after a month-long hospitalization with pneumonia, Patsy Takemoto Mink died in Honolulu. Her name had already been put on the ballot for re-election, and she won posthumously. Her signature Title IX legislation was renamed in her honor: the Patsy T. Mink Equal Opportunity in Education Act. In 2014, she was given the Presidential Medal of Freedom, the nation's highest civilian honor.

MARSHA P. JOHNSON

(1945–1992)

In June 2014, President Barack Obama designated the Stonewall National Monument as the newest addition to America's National Park System, saying, "Stonewall will be our first national monument to tell the story of the struggle for LGBT rights. I believe our national parks should reflect the full story of our country, the richness and diversity and uniquely American spirit that has always defined us. That we are stronger together. That out of many, we are one." Forty-five years earlier, women like Marsha P. Johnson were among those who risked their lives fighting to draw attention to the rights of the LGBTQ community.

Marsha was born Malcolm Michaels Jr. on August 24, 1945, in Elizabeth, New Jersey. She was the fifth child of seven to Malcolm Michaels Sr., a General Motors factory worker, and Alberta Claiborne, a housekeeper. When Marsha was around 5 years old, she began to wear dresses. When her peers responded aggressively, she stopped. Her family regularly attended the Mount Teman African Methodist Episcopal Church, and Marsha connected with Christianity. Inside, she knew she was attracted to men, but as a devout Christian she couldn't imagine a life in which she could act on those feelings. Immediately after graduating from Thomas A. Edison High School in 1963, she moved to New York City with just $15 and a bag of clothes.

Upon her arrival in New York, she began using the name Black Marsha. Marsha referred to herself as a transvestite (the common term of the time, rather than trans or transgender) and used she/her pronouns. But most of all, Marsha said, "I think of myself as me." There were still many laws against "sexual deviancy" in the 1960s, including same-sex dancing in public, cross-dressing, and even serving LGBTQ people alcoholic beverages. This forced people like Marsha, who were determined to live authentically, to dwell on the outskirts of society. To get by, Marsha waited tables, but she later turned to panhandling (her signature phrase was, "Spare change for a dying queen") and prostitution as a means of survival. She became a staple of Greenwich Village, a neighborhood central to the LGBTQ community.

Early in Marsha's time in New York, she met Sylvia Rivera, a precocious 11-year-old who grew up to be one of her best friends and collaborators. Marsha already thought of herself as an "old queen"—presumably life on the street in 1960s Greenwich Village aged a person quickly—and her heart went out to Sylvia. She took Sylvia under her wing and taught her how to panhandle. For the rest of the decade, they stuck together, dreaming about the day LGBTQ citizens would have the same rights as straight people.

On June 28, 1969, a riot broke out at the Stonewall Inn, a prominent gay bar on Christopher Street in Greenwich Village. It was one of the few places that served alcohol to LGBTQ folks, but the police consistently raided the bar for doing so—in fact, they had raided just the night before. Marsha, then 23, had been there when the police lined everyone up against the bar and searched them. The next night, however, the patrons decided they had had enough of the arbitrary discrimination and harassment, and they staged an uprising. Stonewall patrons resisted inside the bar until the protest spread outside to the street, at which point the police set the Stonewall on fire. Marsha arrived around 2 a.m. and quickly joined the fight, which had turned physical, with patrons throwing bottles, stones, and anything else they could get their hands on at the police. The patrons turned over cars, shouting against police brutality. Marsha reportedly climbed a lamppost and dropped a heavy object onto the windshield of a cop car. The protests continued for the next six days.

Marsha and Sylvia emerged from Stonewall as leaders of the gay liberation movement. (In those days, "gay" was an umbrella term for all LGBTQ identifications, similar to the way "queer" is used today.) The night after the rebellion, Marsha helped form the Gay Liberation Front (GLF) and the group met on the steps of Stonewall, setting into motion a series of small revolutions. Over the next year, the GLF announced its presence, handing out leaflets, sharing medical and legal information affecting the queer community, and starting the first LGBTQ community center. On the first anniversary of Stonewall, June 28, 1970, the GLF organized Christopher Street Liberation Day, the first ever gay pride march and, incredibly, one of three marches organized in cities across the United States that year. The Christopher Street Liberation Day march stretched from the Stonewall Inn up Sixth Avenue and to Central Park.

That year, the GLF protested New York University, which had canceled gay dances at Weinstein Residence Hall, by holding a five-day sit-in in the dormitory. After the NYU protest, Sylvia and Marsha founded Street Transvestite Action Revolutionaries (STAR), to advocate and create a community for trans youth and, specifically, to shelter kids who weren't safe at home. STAR was likely the first US organization led by trans women of color. At the first meeting, Sylvia asked Marsha to be president, but Marsha felt the role was outside her abilities and accepted the position of vice president instead. The group set up the first LGBTQ youth shelter in North America on East Second Street, called STAR House, providing meals and clothes as well as shelter. The shelter was short-lived, but the organization lasted until 1973.

Marsha's style came into its own in the 1970s, featuring bright wigs, flowers (real or plastic) in her hair, and bold costume jewelry. Many of the materials that went into her outfits she scavenged from the street. Marsha's cheerful, loving demeanor also drew people to her, which was a powerful tool for her activism. When asked what the *P* in her name stood for, she always said, "Pay it no mind!" Marsha's friends saw her as extraordinarily sweet and generous. As an extension of her embrace of femininity, in 1972 Marsha began performing drag with the performance group Hot Peaches, and continued doing so for the rest of her life. Andy Warhol took portraits of Marsha for his 1975 "Ladies and Gentleman" portfolio, which depicted drag queen culture and its subversion of the gender binary.

Marsha had her first mental breakdown in 1970; by 1979, she had experienced several more. Even when Marsha was not experiencing a psychiatric crisis, she was sometimes incoherent and suffered hallucinations. She also took on a male persona, Malcolm, who could be violent—entirely the opposite of the loving, joyful Marsha.

Marsha's encounters with the police didn't end with Stonewall. She claimed she stopped counting her arrests after the first 100. She frequently spent time in jail, and she faced life-threatening situations as a prostitute who was also often homeless. All this made her more determined than ever to advocate for those who needed protection, especially homeless trans youth.

In the 1980 Gay Pride parade in New York City, the LGBTQ community honored Marsha by inviting her to ride in the parade's lead car. The same year, she began living with her friend Randy Wicker, a gay activist she had met in 1973 when he was a journalist for *The Advocate*.

When the AIDS epidemic swept through her community in the 1980s, Marsha focused on bringing attention to the disease. She participated with AIDS Coalition to Unleash Power (ACT UP). Overcome with grief as she lost friends to the disease, including Randy's partner, David Combs, Marsha spent time in solitude at the Catholic Community of Saints Peter and Paul church near her home in Hoboken, New Jersey. In a June 26, 1992, interview, Marsha revealed that she'd been HIV-positive for two years. Two days later, she celebrated Pride for the 22nd year.

Marsha's cheerful, loving demeanor also drew people to her, which was a powerful tool for her activism. When asked what the *P* in her name stood for, she always said, "Pay it no mind!"

The 1992 parade was one of the last times Marsha was seen. Her body was found floating in the Hudson River on July 6, 1992, near the Christopher Street Pier. Marsha P. Johnson was 46 years old. The police quickly ruled her death a suicide, but her friends and family protested: Marsha had shown no signs of suicidal ideation, and just two days prior to her disappearance she had told friends that a car had been following her. During Marsha's funeral procession, mourners marched through the streets to the Hudson River spot where her body was found. Randy and Sylvia spread Marsha's ashes over the water. Sylvia later said of Marsha's death, "When she died, part of me went with her. . . . One of our pacts was that we would always cross the River Jordan together, and to me, this is the River Jordan: the Hudson River."

Later, the NYPD changed Marsha's cause of death from suicide to undetermined, and in 2012 they reopened the case. A documentary exploring a trans activist's pursuit of Marsha's cold case, *The Death and Life of Marsha P. Johnson*, was released in 2017. In the film, part of Marsha's autopsy report was obtained, and it noted that her death was possibly a homicide.

Marsha's legacy lives on through the Marsha P. Johnson Institute and activists fighting for LGBTQ equality around the world. Some have called her a saint. In 2019, New York City announced it would be creating a monument in honor of Marsha and Sylvia near the Stonewall Inn for their pioneering work as advocates for trans rights and acceptance.

ELIZABETH JENNINGS

(c. 1826–1901)

A century before Rosa Parks refused to give up her bus seat, a 24-year-old teacher laid the groundwork by refusing to get off a streetcar. Forty-one years later, that same courageous woman founded New York City's first public kindergarten for black children.

There are conflicting records of the date of Elizabeth Jennings' birth. The 1850 US Census states she was born in 1830, but her death certificate in 1901 lists her birth year as 1826. She was born in Manhattan to Elizabeth Cartwright Jennings and Thomas L. Jennings. Her maternal grandfather, Jacob Cartwright, was a native African who served in the Revolutionary War before taking part in New York City politics. Elizabeth's father was a respected abolitionist, also involved in politics, and a successful tailor who earned a patent for a mending invention—the first patent in the United States awarded to a black person. He was born free and served in the War of 1812. Elizabeth's parents ran a boarding-house at 167 Church Street, part of Manhattan's Fifth Ward, where their family also lived. Elizabeth had two brothers and one sister: Thomas, William, and Matilda.

From the get-go, Elizabeth was intelligent, hardworking, and passionate about learning. She went to the local Colored Normal School, where she learned English and grammar, US history, algebra and geometry, astronomy, and philosophy. She earned her diploma from the New York Board of Education and set out to become a teacher, a common occupation for black women. She was unmarried, so Elizabeth continued living with her family at their boardinghouse.

She began teaching in 1848 in the girls' department of Colored Public School No. 2, which was operated by the Public School Society, before going to work in the boys' department at the same school in fall 1849, which was operated by the New York Society for the Promotion of Education among Colored Children. Even though less than 2 percent of black children were enrolled in schools, the city had four separate agencies running them: the Public School Society, the Board of Education of the City and County of New York, the New York Colored Orphan Asylum, and the New York Society for the Promotion of Education among Colored Children.

The following year, Elizabeth was transferred to the Promotion Society's School No. 1, which was located in the undercroft of St. Philip's Church. It was smaller than School No. 2, which had 268 students. Her salary was $225 a year. In July 1851, the school's principal, Samuel Vreeland Berry, resigned. Elizabeth began the school year as the acting principal. She didn't receive a raise for the promotion, but she was given two assistants. In 1852, she returned to teaching (with the same salary) this time in the boys' department. The school's principal was Charles L. Reason, a conductor in the Underground Railroad. His salary was $450, double what Elizabeth had earned in her time as principal.

Elizabeth was also involved with her church, the First Colored American Congregational Church on Sixth Street near the Bowery, which was active in the abolitionist movement. Elizabeth served as the organist and played during services every Sunday. In addition to religious sermons, the church also featured lectures like "Elevation of the African Race" and "The Duty of Colored People Towards the Overthrow of American Slavery."

In 1854, both the Society for the Promotion of Education among Colored Children and the Public School Society went out of business. The City of New York formed a Board of Education to take over its schools and maintain student attendance. Elizabeth remained teaching in the boys' department of Colored School No. 5 for $225 a year until 1857.

On July 16, 1854, Elizabeth was running late to play organ at her church. She and her friend Sarah Adams hailed a horse-drawn streetcar at the corner of Pearl and Chatham Streets (Park Row today). Streetcars weren't officially segregated, but some had signs that said "Colored People Allowed In This Car," and it was customary for black passengers to leave the car if a white passenger objected to their presence. The streetcar that Elizabeth and Sarah hailed didn't have a sign, but when they tried to board, the Irish-born conductor told them to wait for the next car, which Elizabeth recalled him saying "had her people in it." Elizabeth responded that she was running late for church and couldn't wait and that she "had no people." She was 24.

The conductor insisted that Elizabeth and Sarah get off the streetcar, but Elizabeth replied that she would wait until the next car came up. When it arrived, the driver told Elizabeth the streetcar was full and she should stay on the car she had already boarded. That conductor continued to insist that Elizabeth and

Sarah get off. For a few minutes, he attempted to wait them out, but he soon grew impatient. At that point, the driver allowed them on but warned them, "If the passengers raise any objections, you shall go out." Elizabeth, offended, told him she had "never been insulted before going to church."

The conductor told Elizabeth and Sarah he would remove them from the car himself. First, he took Sarah from the car as she screamed for him to let her go. Elizabeth told the conductor "not to lay his hands" on her, but he seized her anyway. She grabbed the window sash and held on as he pulled her. When the conductor wasn't able to remove her, he ordered the driver to tie up the horses and assist. The two of them seized a screaming Elizabeth by the arms and dragged her down the stairs onto street level, with her head toward the ground and her legs in the air. Sarah stood by, yelling, "You'll kill her. Don't kill her."

When the men let go of Elizabeth, she got right back in the streetcar. The conductor told her, "You shall sweat for this," and instructed the driver to go as fast as he could and not to stop until he saw a police officer or station. They encountered an officer at the corner of Walker and Bowery. He boarded the streetcar and, without listening to a word Elizabeth had to say, grabbed her and shoved her out of the streetcar. Her dress was dirtied, and her bonnet fell off and was crushed. The officer "tauntingly told [her] to get redress if [she] could" and "drove [her] away like a dog" from the streetcar, warning her not to start a mob or a fight.

The next day, the reverends at Elizabeth's church gathered their parishioners together to hear her story. She wrote a statement, which the church secretary read aloud on her behalf (the preceding quotes above are from that statement). Elizabeth didn't attend because she was "quite sore and stiff from the treatment [she] received from these monsters in human form yesterday afternoon." Those who heard her statement were outraged on her behalf. They resolved to form a committee to "bring the whole affair before the legal authorities" and demand that the proprietors, the Third Avenue Railway Company, provide an equal right to transit. Black newspapers reported Elizabeth's story, and she received support from around the country.

Elizabeth's father, Thomas, and fellow abolitionists brought Elizabeth's case to the law offices of Culver, Parker, and Arthur, a white firm, stating the case would be on behalf of all black New Yorkers. Erastus Culver, the head of the firm, was a widely known abolitionist who had been a featured speaker at meetings of the New York Anti-Slavery Society. The firm had a reputation for representing abolitionist cases. Culver assigned the case to a new addition to the firm who had just passed the bar exam a few months earlier: Chester A. Arthur, later to become the 21st president of the United States. He was 24 years old at the time—about the same age as Elizabeth—and although he was young, he already had a reputation for his abolitionist senti-ments. He'd written an anti-slavery essay in college, and in 1852, as a clerk for Culver, he participated in a fugitive slave case that successfully argued slaves transported across New York state lines, where slavery was outlawed in 1827, would be freed.

The conductor and driver seized a screaming Elizabeth by the arms and dragged her off the street car with her legs in the air. Her friend Sarah stood by, yelling, "You'll kill her. Don't kill her."

Once Elizabeth had recovered from her injury she went back to work at Colored Public School No. 2 and resumed her organist duties at church.

The Third Avenue Railway Company was headquartered in Brooklyn, so Elizabeth's case was argued in the Brooklyn Cir-cuit of the New York State Supreme Court on February 22, 1855. Elizabeth sued the company for $500 in damages, which would be about $15,000 in today's money. Chester Arthur argued in front of Judge William Rockwell that a recently enacted New York state law made common carriers (i.e., public transportation) liable for their employees' actions. Judge Rockwell agreed and ruled in Elizabeth's favor. The jury, which was all male and all white, agreed, but didn't give Elizabeth the full $500 she sought. They awarded her only $225 plus $22.50 in costs—about the same as her annual salary.

The black community cheered the success of Elizabeth's case, which was seen as an important legal precedent. The *New York Tribune* stated, "It is high time the rights of this class of citizens were ascertained," and Frederick Douglass himself wrote in *Frederick Douglass' Paper*, "We hold our New York City gentlemen responsible for the carrying out of this decision into practice by putting an end to their exclusion from cars and omnibuses." Other black men and women were thrown off streetcars after Elizabeth's case concluded, and if they brought lawsuits, not all were as lucky as Elizabeth, as the results of their cases often depended on the judge. To keep up the fight against segregation in transportation through litigation, Elizabeth's father founded and was president of the Legal Rights Association.

Around the time of the streetcar incident, the New York Board of Education opened up two schools for additional educational training for teachers. Classes were all day on Saturdays, but Elizabeth jumped at the chance. By 1859, she had an additional diploma and was called "the most learned of our female teachers in the city of New York" in *Frederick Douglass' Paper*.

Elizabeth experienced a devastating loss when her father passed away on February 11, 1859. He was 68 years old and had been her greatest champion. Other prominent members of the black community eulogized him, including Frederick Douglass.

After 12 years of teaching, Elizabeth finally got a $25 raise in 1860, bringing her salary up to $275 a year. In June of the same year, she married Charles Graham. The Board of Education had laws stating that a woman could be let go from her job once she married, but Elizabeth continued working at Colored School No. 5 under her married name, Elizabeth Jennings Graham. The couple lived together at 541 Broome Street, where her mother continued to operate a boardinghouse. That fall, Abraham Lincoln was elected the sixteenth president of the United States, and a month after that, the first state seceded from the Union.

Meanwhile, through her father's Legal Rights Association, other black New Yorkers continued to challenge segregation in the courts. In 1873, the New York State Legislature passed the Civil Rights Act of 1873, making openly discriminatory public transit illegal. Although he didn't live to see the results, Elizabeth's father and his Legal Rights Association's strategy of using litigation to challenge injustice became a model for furthering civil rights in the 20th century.

In 1862, Elizabeth got another raise, to $300 a year. She and Charles also had a son, Thomas L. They likely adopted him, as there are no records of his birth and no evidence of Elizabeth taking time off from work to give birth.

From July 13 to July 17, 1863, New York City experienced riots that resulted in 120 dead, 2,000 injured, and millions of dollars in damage. The Union Conscription Act passed that February, which made it possible for all able-bodied men between the ages of 20 and 45 to be drafted into service for the Union Army in their fight against the Confederacy. It was the first mandatory draft instituted in the United States, but it excluded rich men, who could buy their way out of service for $300, and black men, who weren't considered citizens. Poor white men felt unfairly targeted. On July 11, the first lottery for the draft began, picking the names of the men who'd be conscripted into service. On the second day, only a few names were called before the city exploded into riots, mainly Irish immigrants targeting the black population. The riots were finally stopped by Union soldiers returning from the Battle of Gettysburg. Of the 120 killed, 105 were black New Yorkers, and more than 5,000 were left homeless.

On the fourth day of the rioting, Elizabeth and Charles' son died of "convulsions." He was only 1 year old. With the rioting officially over but some lingering violence in the area, they buried their only child in the St. Philip's Church section at Cypress Hills Cemetery in Brooklyn on July 20, 1863.

Despite this tragedy, there are no records at the Board of Education that Elizabeth took any time off work. When school started again in the fall, she was back at Colored School No. 5 working full time. The following school year, the boys' and girls'

The New York Board of Education opened up two schools for additional educational training. Classes were all day on Saturdays, but Elizabeth jumped at the chance. By 1859, she had an additional diploma and was called "the most learned of our female teachers in the city of New York" in the *Frederick Douglass' Paper*.

departments were combined. A year later, Elizabeth likely left the public school system and went into private teaching.

Charles passed away in 1867.

In 1881, Elizabeth was suddenly back in the national conversation when US Vice President Chester A. Arthur became president after James A. Garfield was assassinated. As the nation read about their new leader, they learned he'd long been a "champion among colored people" since his participation in the "Lizzie Jennings" case. There's nothing to suggest that Elizabeth had kept in touch with her lawyer 25 years later, and she never publicly commented on her opinion of him, even though she was no stranger to writing in to the black newspapers of the day.

By 1890, Elizabeth, now in her sixties, moved uptown to 237 West 41st Street, part of a larger black migration as New York City extended north into the island of Manhattan. In 1895, she converted the bottom floor of her home into the first public kindergarten for black children in the city. Called the Free Kindergarten Association for Colored Children, it contained a desk-filled classroom and a lending library filled with books donated by some of the well-known benefactors of the school, including W.E.B. DuBois. The walls were covered in the children's artwork, and there was a yard outside where they tended a garden and played. Elizabeth had the help of several women in running the school, which also hosted a sewing school on Saturdays for people of all ages.

Six years after she founded her school, Elizabeth Jennings Graham quietly passed away in her home above the school on June 5, 1901, at about age 75. She succumbed to complications of Bright's disease, which affects the kidneys, after some time in a coma. She was buried near her son in Cypress Hills Cemetery.

Before the Civil War, Elizabeth Jennings Graham was already setting a precedent for the fight for civil rights that would continue for more than a century. Beyond that, however, she spent her life as an educator and advocate for the black community. Until recently, historians largely overlooked her contributions. In 2007, a classroom at P.S. 361 in Manhattan successfully lobbied for a street sign that reads "Elizabeth Jennings Place" at Spruce Street and Park Row, near where the streetcar incident occurred. And in March 2019, the city of New York announced it would install a monument to Elizabeth in Grand Central Terminal. Elizabeth's courage to stand up for herself in a time when slavery was still legal led to the desegregation of New York City's public transportation, perhaps sooner than it would have otherwise. This action was emblematic of her life, which she spent working for the improvement of New York's black community.

PART THREE

THE CEILING BREAKERS

Women who dare to take up space in male-dominated
fields face many challenges. But their courage
can have reverberating effects, pushing open the
doors of opportunity—even if just a crack—for
the women who follow behind them.

MADAM
C.J. WALKER

(1867–1919)

Madam C.J. Walker lived a rags-to-riches life right out of a fairy tale. She was orphaned before her 10th birthday, and by age 20, she was a widowed laundress struggling to keep a roof over her family's head. At the time of her death, she was a world-traveling philanthropist whose company empowered women through the use of its hair-care products and by training them for careers of their own. The first woman millionaire in the United States was not only self-made, she was also a single black mother only a generation out of slavery.

Madam C.J. Walker was born Sarah Breedlove on December 23, 1867, a few years after the end of slavery. Madam was born on the former Burney plantation in Delta, Louisiana, where her parents, once slaves, were sharecroppers. She was the Breedloves' fifth child and the first born free.

Madam began helping out in the cotton fields at a very young age, and later told a reporter she had only three months of formal schooling. Her mother passed away when she was 6, and her father a year later, leaving Madam in the care of her oldest sister, Louvenia Powell, and her husband, Jesse.

After a bad cotton harvest in 1878, the family joined the girls' brother Alexander across the Mississippi River in Vicksburg, Mississippi. Louvenia's husband saw Madam as a burden, so 11-year-old Madam joined Louvenia in finding work as a laundress.

When she was just 14, Madam met and married Moses McWilliams. She later spoke of her first marriage in practical, unsentimental terms: "I married at the age of fourteen in order to get a home of my own." Three years later, on June 6, 1885, their daughter, Lelia, was born.

When Lelia was just 3 years old, Moses McWilliams died. Although she was a 20-year-old single mother with limited resources, Madam refused to move back in with her cruel brother-in-law. Madam and Lelia traveled north to St. Louis, Missouri, where several of her brothers had opened a barbershop.

Madam took work as a washerwoman, doing the laundry by hand for two or three white families and earning as little as $1.50 per day for the work. On Sundays, her only day away from the washtub, Madam visited the St. Paul American Methodist Episcopal (AME) Church one block from her brothers' barbershop. Through the church, the St. Louis Colored Orphans' Home offered to allow Lelia, a "half-orphan," to live at the orphanage for part of the week. Madam accepted, although it's unclear how long this arrangement was in place.

Madam and Leila moved frequently, sometimes twice or more in a single year, barely avoiding homelessness. They remained in the same neighborhood from 1891 to 1896, however, so Lelia consistently attended the same elementary school. Madam became involved with a man named John Davis, who was new to St. Louis. He moved in with Madam and 9-year-old Lelia in spring 1894, and that August, they were married at city hall. Madam was 27—still young, but nearly double her age when she first married. Madam quickly learned that John was happy to share in her earnings and spend the money at the local bars. He came home drunk and hit her. Soon he was openly flaunting his girlfriend.

Around this time, Madam discovered that her hair was beginning to fall out. This was a common complaint for black women; it was difficult to have healthy hair in the 1890s. Women typically washed their hair only once a month, which caused scalp disease. Harsh treatments to combat the condition, plus malnutrition and stress, often led to hair loss. She began to experiment with over-the-counter hair treatments.

By 1896, Madam's longtime St. Louis neighborhood had devolved into one of the worst in the city. Madam and her extended family moved to the nearby neighborhood of Mill Creek Valley, although they maintained their involvement with St. Paul AME Church. Madam was strict about Leila continuing to attend school.

In November 1903, John Davis reported that Madam had deserted him. This was not a tragedy for Madam or Lelia; in fact, Madam had begun seeing a new beau. Charles Joseph "C.J." Walker was a well-dressed "newsman" who likely sold subscriptions and advertising. Madam liked C.J.'s ambition and drive, and she thought that, unlike John Davis, this man could help improve her standing. Madam also began taking classes at night school and volunteering with the St. Paul AME Church, helping those as needy as she had been.

Madam also began working as a sales agent for Annie Pope-Turnbo, who produced a line of hair-care products for black women. Madam saw a future in hairdressing. It was far less laborious than laundry, with the opportunity to earn double the salary. Pope-Turnbo's products, and her method of regular shampooing and scalp massage, cured Madam's scalp issues, and her hair started growing back. Madam loved helping women feel better about themselves, which could in turn lead them to improved financial opportunities, as it did for her.

Madam decided to make a home in Denver, Colorado. On July 19, 1905, Madam boarded a train and traveled nearly 900 miles west with a bag full of Annie Pope-Turnbo's Wonderful Hair Grower. She was 37 years old, and the rest of her life was just beginning.

Madam found a job earning $30 a month as a cook in a boardinghouse. She joined the local chapter of the AME Church

Madam saw a future in hairdressing. It was far less laborious than laundry, with the opportunity to earn double the salary.

and continued selling Pope-Turnbo's line. The black community in Denver was small and close-knit, and soon the products were a hit. So was Madam.

One of the tenants at the boardinghouse owned the local pharmacy. Madam had him analyze Annie Pope-Turnbo's product and uncover its formula. It wasn't an entirely original product—variations had been around since at least the 16th century. Madam was soon using her free time to develop her own version. After a few months, she saved up enough money to quit her job, rent an attic room as a laboratory, and work just two days a week as a washerwoman. The other five days she spent doing hair treatments with Pope-Turnbo's product while developing her own. In December 1905, she placed her first advertisement in the local black newspaper, *The Statesman*: "Mrs. McWilliams, formerly of St. Louis, has special rates for a month to demonstrate her ability to grow hair."

C.J. followed Madam to Denver, and on January 4, 1906, they were married by the pastor of the local AME church. In March 1906, Madam updated her newspaper advertisements to call herself "Mrs. C.J. Walker."

Madam began to travel to nearby cities to spread the word about her (or, for the time being, Annie Pope-Turnbo's) magical hair products. Madam's ads included a photograph of her own hair as proof that the treatment worked.

In May 1906, Madam abruptly ceased advertising her services using Pope-Turnbo's products, and in late July, she reemerged as Madam C.J. Walker, with her own offering. It was unusual for black women to be addressed as Madam or by their last name. Instead, they were referred to as Aunt or Auntie and their first name. This distinction gave the Madam C.J. Walker Manufacturing Company an air of sophistication. She began to use the name everywhere.

In addition to the new name, Madam fashioned a new origin story for herself in which she never married John Davis or worked for Annie Pope-Turnbo.

Madam began training women in the cities around Denver to implement her hair treatments. She offered an affordable course for women to become a Walker agent, aiming to grow her own business while helping poorer women increase their earnings. Lelia arrived in Denver to help out. Madam introduced her around town, then she and C.J. traveled to the South to spread the word about the company. Leila took charge of the Denver operation.

On the road, Madam and C.J. developed a routine. They would contact the local AME church, find the nicest affordable boardinghouse (few hotels welcomed black guests), and introduce themselves to the local black organizations. They would host a demonstration of their specialty hair grower product at a church or lodge and hold classes to train local agents in the "Walker method"—vigorous brushing and the application of heated iron combs to the hair in order to transform stubborn lusterless hair into shining smoothness. Sometimes they wrote ahead to the leaders of the local black organizations and secured a place to stay through them. They systematically made their way through the South, passing through 90 percent of the nation's black population at the time, in only 18 months. By May 1907, Lelia closed up shop in Denver on Madam and C.J.'s orders, as they had determined Denver was too small a market to spend so much time on. With requests coming in from coast to coast, the Walkers realized the business had grown too big for them to continue selling door-to-door. It was a smash success. That first year on the road, Madam brought in $3,652, which was likely equal to her total lifetime earnings as a washerwoman.

Madam and C.J. set up temporary headquarters in Pittsburgh, Pennsylvania. Sixteen different rail lines could easily reach any destination in the country, which would be beneficial to their burgeoning mail-order business. Pittsburgh had no black newspaper in which to advertise, so Madam sought endorsements from local black leadership. She quickly set up the Walker Hair Parlor, later called Lelia College, which trained agents in the Walker method. In 1908, Madam almost doubled her income from the year before.

The Walkers arrived in Indianapolis, Indiana, in February 1910, and within days they decided to make it their new company headquarters. Every day more than 500 trains on eight major rail systems passed through the city, making it an ideal location for building a factory that would ship products across the nation. The city also had a thriving black community. Madam immediately announced her arrival in one of its black newspapers, the *Indianapolis Recorder*. Indianapolis had no beauty parlors like the Walker Parlor, especially for black women, so she showed Indianapolis women what they'd been missing.

Around this time, Madam met Freeman Ransom, a young lawyer who had also moved to Indianapolis recently. She saw in him a highly moral man who could help her run her business. Ransom went on to be her right hand. Madam built a factory and an additional location of Lelia College in Indianapolis. She employed 950 Walker sales agents and more than 30 people in her Indianapolis offices and factory. A month later, she formally incorporated the Madam C.J. Walker Manufacturing Company of Indiana after five years fully in business for herself.

That fall, Madam began to use her fortune to help others in a large-scale way by pledging $1,000 in a publicized campaign to renovate the Indianapolis YMCA. (Julius Rosenwald, president of Sears and Roebuck and friend of Booker T. Washington, offered to contribute $25,000 to any city that raised $75,000 to build a black YMCA.) When announcing her donation at the campaign's launch event, Madam told the crowd, "If the association can save our boys, our girls will be saved, and that's what I'm interested in." The *Indianapolis Freeman*, a nationally read black newspaper founded by former slave George Knox, wrote about her generous donation and published her photo.

Madam believed an endorsement from Booker T. Washington would not only bring her a swell of new customers but also land her in the circle of the highest-regarded black Americans of the day. She wrote to Washington, president of the National Negro Business League, in January 1910, seeking his help in creating a stock offering for the Walker Manufacturing Company. He responded that although he wished her success, he was too busy to take on the project. In late 1911, she wrote to him again, requesting a speaking slot at his upcoming Negro Farmers' Conference. She believed the audience would find her story uplifting. Washington's reply was blunt: "I fear you misunderstand the kind of meeting our Tuskegee Negro Conference will be." The weekend of the conference in January 1912, she showed up on Washington's doorstep with a letter of introduction from the executive secretary of the Indianapolis YMCA. Washington relented and allowed her to speak for 10 minutes at the chapel. It was a separate event from the conference, but a win nonetheless. Legend has it that Madam won over Washington's family by demonstrating her hair treatment on his wife and daughters.

That August was Washington's annual National Negro Business League convention. Madam arrived in Chicago determined to speak, although she wasn't on the official roster (two other hair-care entrepreneurs were included, however, and they were likely less successful than Madam). After one of the other purveyors finished, George Knox stood and addressed Washington from the audience: "I arise to ask this convention for a few minutes of its time to hear a remarkable woman. . . . She is the woman who gave $1,000 to the Young Men's Christian Association of Indianapolis. Madam Walker, the lady I refer to, is the manufacturer of hair goods and preparations." But Washington brushed him off—a move that likely shocked the audience, as Knox was a respected guest and this was not an unusual or unreasonable request.

On the last day of the conference, Madam addressed Washington herself. From the audience and between scheduled speakers, she said, "Surely you are not going to shut the door in my face. I have been trying to get before you business people and tell you what I am doing. I am a woman who came from the cotton fields of the South. I was promoted from there to the washtub. Then I was promoted to the cook kitchen, and from there I promoted myself into the business of manufacturing hair goods and preparations. . . . Don't think because you have to go down in the washtub that you are any less a lady!" As she listed her successes, the audience began to clap, but she stopped them: "Please don't applaud—just let me talk!" She concluded, "Now my object in life is not simply to make money for myself or to spend it on myself in dressing or running around in an automobile. But I love to use a part of what I make in trying to help others." Once the applause died down, Washington moved on to the next speaker. Madam may have won over the crowd, but she hadn't officially earned Washington's favor. A few months later, however, she received an invitation to speak at the following year's convention.

Madam returned to Indianapolis from the convention to face the inevitable end of her relationship with C.J., which had been

"If the association can save our boys, our girls will be saved, and that's what I'm interested in."

deteriorating for years. Madam had long suspected that he mismanaged their money, but they also had a fundamental philosophical disagreement over how to spend that money. While Madam wanted to help others, C.J. was most interested in material things. He had also been unfaithful while on the road.

Lelia Walker

(1885–1931)

Lelia Walker, daughter of Madam C.J. Walker, played an integral role in her mother's business, and became its president after her mother's death in 1919. About two years later, she changed her name to A'Lelia and made turbans her signature look. Poet Langston Hughes dubbed her "the joy goddess of Harlem" because she was a vital patron of the Harlem Renaissance. She regularly hosted artists, writers, musicians, and royalty at the Dark Tower, her Harlem salon, and Villa Lewaro, her home on the Hudson.

Single again at 44, Madam turned her attention to her company's future. What would happen after she and Lelia passed on? She found a solution in Fairy Mae Bryant, the 13-year-old daughter of a local Indianapolis widow. Fairy Mae was smart and well-educated for her age, but as part of a large family without an income after the death of her father, she could not afford to attend high school. Fairy Mae was of Native American, African, and European descent, and she wore her long, thick, healthy hair in beautiful braids. In early 1912, Madam asked Fairy Mae's mother for permission to take the girl to Harlem on a modeling trip. Fairy Mae's mother likely welcomed the opportunity for her child to bring in additional income. She did not, however, welcome Madam and Lelia's offer to adopt Fairy Mae. After some resistance, Fairy Mae's mother finally consented, and in late October 1912, two weeks after Madam's divorce from C.J. was finalized, Fairy Mae's adoption was complete. Fairy Mae changed her name to Mae Walker Robinson and became the official heir to the company.

The following summer, in July 1913, the Indianapolis YMCA, to which Madam had pledged $1,000 two years earlier, was finally slated for its grand opening. Booker T. Washington was scheduled to speak at its dedication. Ever determined to win his approval,

Madam invited him to be her houseguest while he was in town, and was thrilled when he accepted. She had the honor of accompanying him to the dedication, where he publicly lauded her generosity. It seemed she had finally won him over.

A few weeks later Madam was booked to speak at the National Negro Business League convention. In Washington's introduction, he called her "one of the most progressive and successful business-women of our race," and after her speech, he remarked, "You talk about what the men are doing in a business way. Why, if we don't watch out, the women will excel us."

That November, Madam set off from New York to the Caribbean and Central America with her niece, Anjetta Breedlove, traveling to the untapped markets of Jamaica, Haiti, Costa Rica, Cuba, and the Panama Canal Zone. While she was there, Lelia and Mae scoped out additional investment properties, including a building in Harlem, a neighborhood which would soon explode as the center of black American cultural life. Lelia spent 1914 renovating the structure (which was designed by Vertner Tandy, one of the first black licensed architects in New York State) into a grand three-floor apartment with a salon on the ground floor.

In 1915, Madam and Mae brought the Walker method to the West Coast. The trip was so successful that Madam decided to extend it by several months. During that time, she was shocked by the news that her hero Washington had passed away. Madam was distraught, writing to Ransom "I have never lost anyone, not even one of my own family, that I regret more than I do the loss of this great and good man."

When Madam and Mae returned to Indianapolis that December, they bid the city goodbye, as Lelia's renovations on the Harlem property were complete. The property combined two buildings into one grand residence. The bottom floor served as the Walker Hair Salon, and the top three floors were the private residence. When Madam arrived in January 1916, she described the ground-floor salon enthusiastically in a letter to Ransom: "[It] beats anything I have ever seen anywhere even in the best hair parlors of the whites." Indianapolis remained the company's headquarters, with Freeman in charge of the day-to-day operations.

New York City was just the place for Madam's growing cultural and political cache. Harlem's growing black community welcomed her with lots of press attention, including one interview where she said, "I first want to say that I did not succeed by traversing a path strewn with roses. I made great sacrifices, met with rebuff after rebuff, and had to fight hard to put my ideas into effect."

A few months later, in early July 1917, a horrific race riot broke out in East St. Louis, Illinois. The riots stemmed from white rage over the employment of black factory workers in the World War I efforts, and it quickly turned into a nightmare for the area's black citizens. Officially, 40 black residents were killed (historians believe the number of victims could be in the hundreds), and an untold number of people were injured. Buildings were destroyed by dozens of fires, and 6,000 black citizens were driven from their homes. President Woodrow Wilson did almost nothing to address the atrocity. The Harlem branch of the NAACP, including Madam and W.E.B. Du Bois, took the train to Washington, DC, with the intention of speaking to the president. This act not only secured Madam's position in the black elite, which was helped by her new home in Harlem, but also solidified her determination to use her position to elevate black Americans.

Soon Madam became fixated on a new innovation for her Walker agents: a union. She saw the potential in organizing the thousands of black women entrepreneurs she'd empowered by passing along the Walker method. Not only could they help each other by exchanging ideas and methods, but they could also harness their collective power on behalf of social causes. Madam tested the waters by organizing the 200 agents in New York into the first chapter of the Madam C.J. Walker Benevolent Association.

On August 31, 1917, the first Madam C.J. Walker Hair Culturists Union of America convention, including more than 200 Walker agents from across the country, gathered in Philadelphia. It was one of the first national conventions dedicated to women entrepreneurs.

By the end of August 1916, Madam had signed the deed to a four-and-a-half-acre property in Irvington-on-Hudson, New York, located 20 miles north of Manhattan. It was the wealthiest neighborhood in the United States. Madam's future neighbors included titans of the age like the Rockefellers, Vanderbilts, and Astors. When news of her home purchase leaked to the press in December 1916, the neighbors were scandalized, but as the house came together, they could not deny that its stateliness fit right in. As construction went on, Madam and Lelia made frequent visits to the property. On one trip, Lelia brought Italian opera singer Enrico Caruso. The property reminded him so much of his native Italy that he called the home Villa Lewaro, "Lewaro" being an acronym of the first two letters in each word of Lelia's married name, Lelia Walker Robinson. The name stuck.

Villa Lewaro was finished just as Madam needed to rest. In late 1917, while she was on the road, she fell ill and was diagnosed with nephritis, an acute inflammation of the kidneys. Doctors recommended she stop working, but Madam couldn't bear the inactivity for long. By late summer 1918, she was back at Villa Lewaro resting out of necessity. She remained there through the fall and spent Christmas and her birthday surrounded by family and friends. In February 1919, her doctor, who'd served in World War I, returned from France. He noted that her kidney disease had advanced significantly. Madam rested for about a month, but then went on a Midwest sales trip, revisiting the cities in which she'd spent most of her life, Indianapolis and St. Louis.

On Good Friday, April 25, staying with friends from her St. Louis days, Madam became so sick that she told a friend she only had a short time to live. She departed for Villa Lewaro that Monday, with a St. Louis doctor monitoring her condition during the train ride. Once home, she worked with Ransom to draft her will, purchased $4,000 in Victory Bonds (which helped pay for the war), and told the NAACP she'd be pledging $5,000 to their anti-lynching campaign. She minimized her sickness to Lelia and Mae, who were abroad on a sales trip to Cuba, so they did not come home. On May 24, 1919, she slipped into a coma. She died the following day, at age 51. Lelia and Mae were on a ship back to New York when they heard the news of her passing, and they were not back in time for the funeral. Lelia was devastated. Madam was mourned in newspapers the world over. The *New York Times* titled her obituary, "Wealthiest Negress Dead," and many obituaries claimed she was the first female self-made millionaire. It's true Madam was one of the wealthiest women of her time—likely the wealthiest black woman in the United States—and her fortune, if translated to today's dollars, would be in the millions (possibly up to $7 million). However, although she likely earned more than $1 million, between spending and philanthropy, she probably had about $600,000 in assets at the time of her death.

Today, Villa Lewaro and the Madam Walker Theatre Center in Indianapolis, the former factory property, are National Historic Landmarks. In 1998, a US 32-cent stamp honored Madam. On July 20, 2019, West 136th Street in Harlem, the street on which Madam and Lelia's Harlem apartment was located, was renamed Madam C.J. and A'Lelia Walker Place. In 2001, Madam's great-great-granddaughter, A'Lelia Bundles, published a biography of Madam Walker titled *On Her Own Ground: The Life and Times of Madam C.J. Walker*. The book was been adapted for a 2020 Netflix limited series starring Octavia Spencer and Tiffany Haddish as the mother-daughter duo.

Grace Hopper

(1906–1992)

The pioneering computer programmer Grace Hopper is credited with making computers more accessible. She was born Grace Brewster Murray on December 9, 1906, in New York City and was the eldest of three children. Her family instilled a love of learning from a young age. Trained as a mathematician, she graduated from Vassar College in 1928. She took on a teaching post there while pursuing graduate studies at Yale, receiving her master's in 1930 and her Ph.D. in 1934. In 1930, she married New York University literature professor Vincent Foster Hopper; they divorced in 1945 and she never remarried. In December 1943, Grace took a leave of absence from Vassar and enlisted in the U.S. Navy to join the war effort. She was 36 years old. She was assigned to the Bureau of Ordinance Computation Project at Harvard, where the Mark I, one of the earliest computers, was located. Grace became one of its first three programmers and authored a 500-page manual for the machine, which laid the foundation for its operation.

After the war, Grace remained at Harvard, where she helped develop the Mark II and Mark III computers. One August night in 1945, a moth got inside the computer, leading Grace to coin the computer terms "bug" and "debugging." In 1949, she joined the Eckert-Mauchly Computer Corporation in Philadelphia, Pennsylvania, which became Sperry Rand after several acquisitions. There, she worked on the UNIVAC I (Universal Automatic Computer), writing the first compiler, a program that lets users create computer languages that more closely resemble the written word. She also helped develop Flow-Matic, the first English-language compiler.

In the 1960s, Grace advocated for COBOL, or common business-oriented language, which would make computers more accessible to the average person. She saw a future where computers would be a part of everyday life.

Grace retired from the Navy Reserves in 1966 but was quickly called back to active duty the following year to help standardize the Navy's computer languages. She was 60 years old and remained in service for 19 more years. In December 1983, she was promoted to commodore; two years later, her rank was merged with rear admiral, and she became Admiral Grace Hopper. She finally retired at the age of 79, the oldest officer on active duty. But Grace didn't stop working: She went back to the private sector, consulting for the Digital Equipment Corporation. She worked until her death on January 1, 1992, at age 85, at her home in Arlington, Virginia. She was buried with full military honors at Arlington National Cemetery. She received many awards throughout her illustrious career, including a National Medal of Technology and, posthumously, the Presidential Medal of Freedom in 2016. Today, Grace's memory is honored by the annual Grace Hopper Celebration, a conference dedicated to women in STEM.

MARÍA TERESA FERRARI DE GAUDINO

(1887–1956)

María Teresa Ferrari de Gaudino was not going to sit idly and let life pass her by, although for a woman of her social standing, that would have been perfectly respectable. The first woman university professor in all of Latin America was passionate about using her position to champion women's rights and expand knowledge around women's health.

María Teresa Ferrari was born on October 11, 1887, in Buenos Aires, Argentina, to David Ferrari White and Catalina Alvarado. Both sides of her family had connections to the revolution for freedom from Spain. Her paternal great-great-grandfather was Guillermo Pío White, born William Porter White in Pittsfield, Massachusetts. He became a merchant, and after some time in London, moved to Buenos Aires, where he helped finance the war against Spain (possibly for dubious reasons on behalf of the British government). Her maternal great-grandfather, Rudecindo Alvarado, was a hero of the war for independence (receiving commendations from Simon Bolívar himself), and he later became governor of the Argentine province of Salta and briefly served as Argentina's minister of war and the navy.

By María Teresa's generation, the Ferrari family was well-off and well-positioned. Women typically stayed home as wives and mothers; jobs were for those who needed money. Daughters of wealthier families were educated for the sole purpose of succeeding in their domestic destiny. María Teresa earned her teaching degree in 1903. Teaching was a socially acceptable vocation, as it was seen as an extension of a woman's maternal duty.

The following year, she was one of its first women to graduate from the National College of Buenos Aires, after which she entered the Faculty of Medicine at the University of Buenos Aires with the goal of becoming a doctor. Cecilia Grierson, also from Argentina, was the first woman doctor in Latin America; she graduated from medical school in 1889. María Teresa was one of five women in the school at the time. She later said, "We were five girls who were willing to overcome all obstacles." She started teaching psychology at Normal School No. 3 while still in medical school. It was rare for women to attend university, let alone medical school, and to work, so it was quite unusual for a woman to do both simultaneously. Many believed women's participation in the labor market could only lead to further expansion of women's rights in society, which, some worried, could upend the status quo.

María Teresa interned at the Obstetric and Gynecological Clinic of the San Roque Hospital. For her thesis, she studied how pituitary medication affected pregnancies, and her work was published in the medical journal *La Semana Médica*. When María Teresa graduated from medical school in 1911, she was one of the first women to do so in all of Latin America.

Upon receiving her degree, she asked to join the chair of the Obstetric Clinic at the University of Buenos Aires, but the Faculty Teaching Commission denied her request. She responded by saying, "Promote the preparation of women and she will know how to distort the false concepts of her biological inferiority." She became the assistant in the Pathology Department, which allowed her to continue to research. She was in the role for several years, and research became a cornerstone of the rest of her career.

The year after graduating from medical school, María Teresa married Dr. Nicolás M. Gaudino, a urologist who was part of her graduating class. She later described her relationship to a reporter for a 1939 profile: "My husband and I were always great comrades. Together we studied, together we graduated and now we're together later in life. We are partners today as we were when we were students. Our opinions never diverge." By all accounts, Nicolás was an ardent supporter of his wife's ambitions. In 1914, María Teresa was finally admitted to the Obstetric Clinic at the Ramos Mejía Hospital, but when she requested to teach, she was transferred to the Midwives School, which was considered a lower-level institution. Her work at the Midwives School earned her membership to the Society of Obstetrics and Gynecology of Buenos Aires in 1915.

In 1918, María Teresa gave birth to her only child, Mario Nicolás. In the same 1939 interview, she also described raising her son: "I have always personally directed his education, but without hindrance, leaving him free development of his personality. With this I have managed to make my son my best friend." With her home life stable and loving, María Teresa had a strong foundation for pushing professional boundaries.

The year after her son's birth, María Teresa requested permission to enter the contest vying for the vacant alternate professor position in the Faculty of Medicine at the University of Buenos Aires. She had been working at the obstetric clinic for four years. Instead, she was given a "free teacher" position. This may have caused a clash with another doctor at Ramos Mejía Hospital, and she was transferred to a different hospital in late 1920 or early 1921.

In August 1921, she requested a six-month leave of absence to study abroad. Men from wealthy families often continued their training in Europe, but it was rare for a woman to do so. María Teresa thrived in her studies in Paris, visiting different clinics and institutes throughout the city and across Europe. She took a course on radiation with Marie Curie, where she learned about the possibilities of using the new technology to treat genital tumors and uterine fibroids, and she earned a diploma from the Paris School of Medicine.

Upon returning to Argentina, María Teresa was determined to implement the new methods she had learned and bring medical innovations to the women she treated. She faced resistance from her peers, who were not familiar with Madame Curie's work. Instead of performing a total hysterectomy to remove a patient's reproductive organs, María Teresa was able to treat many conditions with radiation, sparing the need for invasive surgery.

"Promote the preparation of women and she will know how to distort the false concepts of her biological inferiority."

Innovating women's health was her passion. In 1924, María Teresa designed an updated vaginoscope that was easy to sterilize, adapted to many speculum models, and allowed doctors to perform well-lit examinations. She presented the invention to the Society of Obstetrics and Gynecology on May 8, 1924, and it made such an impact in the obstetric and gynecological community that she won the Grand Prize at the *Congreso Hispano Lusitano Americano de Ciencias Médicas* (Hispanic American

Lusitano Congress of Medical Sciences) in Seville, Spain, later that year.

The next year, the Central Military Hospital in Buenos Aires called María Teresa to attend a birth by a military wife, as the hospital did not have any obstetricians on staff. She pitched the idea of setting up a maternity ward for the hospital, and in June, thanks to donations, it opened. María Teresa served as the maternity ward's director. Although the military was a male-dominated organization, they seemingly had no issues with granting her a position of power. When the ward launched, the hospital had just one bed for women in labor. In a short amount of time, María Teresa was managing a world-class facility comprising two buildings with forty rooms with single beds, two delivery rooms, a sterilization facility, a recovery room, and an incubator for newborns that provided them with purified air, a unique system in Argentina. Later that year, she was appointed as a delegate of the Argentine government to the First General Congress on Child Welfare in Geneva, Switzerland, as well as a delegate of the Faculty of Medicine to the Medical Days of Rio de Janeiro, in Brazil.

The following year, in October 1926, an alternate professor position opened up in obstetrics in the Faculty of Medical Sciences at the University of Buenos Aires. María Teresa formally put her name in the ring. She had been teaching for more than 20 years in secondary education, had worked as a doctor for 15 years, and had been dedicated to the obstetrics and gynecology specialty even longer, with innovative research published around the globe. For more than a year, the university debated who to hire. Ultimately, an all-male committee had to decide whether to allow women to be promoted. María Teresa had allies fighting on her behalf, arguing there was no rule on the books that prevented hiring a woman and insisting a woman should be hired if she was the best qualified candidate for the job. Finally, on May 12, 1927, the commission in charge of filling the role decided in a vote of 13-2 that "by virtue of the undisputed merits of the applicant, she must be appointed as Alternate Professor." Her proponents denounced the cowardice of

those who had postponed her appointment based on their prejudice or fear of others' criticism.

With that, María Teresa Ferrari de Gaudino became the first
woman professor in all of Latin America. She was 40 years old.
Her appointment was widely covered in the Argentine press, and
it was also written up in newspapers in Italy and Spain, and in US
medical journals. The University of Buenos Aires staff who feared
criticism needn't have worried, as her appointment was largely
celebrated as a step forward for women and the medical profession. In honor of her achievement, her fellow professor and poet
Baldomero Fernández Moreno wrote a poem titled "To Dr. María
Teresa F. de Gaudino," which depicts her in the midst of surgery,
scalpel in hand and blood on her blouse.

On August 1, 1927, a formal event was held at the Federal
Capital Jockey Club in Buenos Aires to welcome María Teresa into
her new role. It was attended by the Minister of the Interior and the
director of the Central Military Hospital (her boss in her role as the
director of the maternity ward), as well as colleagues and friends
in the medical profession. María Teresa gave a speech in which she
said, "I have a fighter temperament in my blood, the energies have
never been lacking, given the conviction that a well-disciplined
intelligence reaches everything that the will proposes."

María Teresa had a full professional plate. In her role as professor, she taught and published her research; at the maternity ward
of the Central Military Hospital, she attended to patients and per-
formed surgeries when necessary; and she still taught psychology
at Normal School No. 3. She published a textbook on obstetrics
during her first year of teaching at the university level and published a paper on "Treatment of Uterine Fibroids by Radiation"
the following year, based on what she had learned from Marie
Curie. She broadened the scope of her research to cover vaccina-
tions and sexually transmitted diseases, especially syphilis. She
attended conferences to present her research and published in
medical journals.

Two years into her role as Alternate Professor, María Teresa
was promoted to Extraordinary Professor of the Obstetric Clinic.

She also embarked on an eight-month study trip across Europe and North America. In January 1930, she attended the VII Latin American Medical Congress in Mexico, where she chaired the first general session and presented three topics relating to obstetrics and gynecology: "Considerations on 40 Cases of Uterine Fibromatosis Treated with Radiation," "Syphilis Ignored," and a third on establishing public clinics to treat syphilis. After the conference, the

> "I have a fighter temperament in my blood, the energies have never been lacking, given the conviction that a well-disciplined intelligence reaches everything that the will proposes."

executive in charge thanked her for her "valuable cooperation for the success of the Congress."

In 1936, after nearly 10 years as a professor, María Teresa created the Argentine Federation of University Women (known as FAMU), with the goal of establishing a better pipeline for women in university society, with recent graduates and older alumni as its members. It was the local chapter of a broader organization based in London known as the International Federation of University Women, which had 80 chapters around the world. She was the group's first president, and she kept the position for 10 years. Many of FAMU's members worked to increase women's rights within Argentine society, focusing on civil and legal rights like the right to vote.

In 1937, María Teresa was given the honor of speaking at the funeral of her predecessor, Dr. Cecilia Grierson. Dr. Grierson had tried and failed to become a medical school professor, but she made countless cracks in the glass ceiling that María Teresa later burst through. That same year, she inaugurated the new maternity pavilion at the Central Military Hospital.

FAMU, and especially María Teresa, also took up the issue of alcoholism. In 1939, María Teresa was invited to speak at the Argentine League Against Alcoholism on alcoholism in women, noting how alcohol adversely affected developing fetuses. That same year, she was promoted to Extraordinary Teacher at the University of Buenos Aires, and in 1940, she stepped down from her role as director of the maternity ward at the Central Military Hospital.

The political scene in Argentina changed in 1946, when Juan Perón became president. The government was announced that Perón sympathizers would fill all positions in the administration. In 1948, María Teresa was asked to step down from her teaching position at the Normal School No. 3 after she refused to contribute to a political collection. She had taught psychology there for 43 years. Argentine women were given the right to vote the following year.

María Teresa continued in her role as a professor of obstetrics and gynecology at the medical school of University of Buenos Aires until she retired on September 15, 1952, at age 65. She had been a professor for 25 years. She wrote in her resignation letter: "I was, in all the universities of Latin America, the first woman who by her own tenacious effort achieved such an honorable distinction that marks in our country the first step towards the equalization of women's rights with those of men. The path that I opened was chosen by many more who opted for my same career and today provide, in general, useful services to the University." Through both her example and FAMU's efforts (which, arguably, was molded in her image), women's representation in universities had increased exponentially.

María Teresa Ferrari de Gaudino died on October 30, 1956. She was 69 years old.

KATE WARNE

(c. 1833–1867)

Sometimes you just have to apply for the job you want, even if you can't fill the usual requirements. Decades before women could join a police force, Kate Warne joined one of the most famous detective agencies in American history. The first female detective paved the way for thousands of women in the police and investigative services—and helped save the life of President Abraham Lincoln in the process.

Kate was born in Erin, a southwestern New York town in Chemung County. Her family was poor, and Kate had to start working at a young age, likely as a housekeeper for wealthier families in town. It's unclear whether Kate was able to attend school, but she likely didn't have much formal education. Still, she developed a fine intellect, and she grew to be graceful and self-possessed, with dark blue eyes described as "filled with fire."

Kate married young, possibly around age 18, and was likely widowed after less than four years of marriage. She did not have children. She moved to Chicago, likely for better employment opportunities.

In 1856, when Kate was about 23, she saw an advertisement in a Chicago newspaper for the Pinkerton National Detective Agency seeking to hire an additional detective. The Pinkerton Agency was founded by Scottish immigrant Allan Pinkerton in 1850, and by 1856, the firm employed nine detectives, all men. We can never know for sure what motivated Kate to seek that position, but she showed up at the Pinkerton offices one afternoon and asked to speak with Allan Pinkerton himself. Kate introduced herself and told him that she was interested in the open detective role. Pinkerton had never heard of a woman detective, but he allowed her to explain why she thought she was a good fit.

Kate believed a woman detective would be able to "go and worm out secrets in many places to which it was impossible for male detectives to gain access" by befriending the wives and mistresses to whom criminals had confided information about their crimes. Men, she explained, might not talk to their friends about their problems, but they turned to women to brag about their successes or to seek solace.

Pinkerton told Kate he would take the night to consider her proposition and asked her to return the next day. He worried that a woman wouldn't be up to the physically demanding work of a detective. One Pinkerton agent once followed a horse-drawn carriage on foot by running after it for 12 miles. But he decided Kate's ideas had merit. The agency was contracted to guard and protect several prominent Midwestern railroads, and part of their contract was to employ assistants with "different qualifications than those [already] in their employ." Pinkerton was interested in solving cases using innovative methods.

Pinkerton later wrote, "I finally became convinced that it would be a good idea to employ her. True, it was the first experiment of the sort that had ever been tried; but we live in a progressive age, and in a progressive country. I therefore determined at least to try it." The next day, Kate returned to Pinkerton's office and secured her place in history as the first woman detective.

Kate was assigned her first case two days into the job, and she quickly proved herself to be a fearless, versatile detective, with great acting skills and strong instincts. She went undercover for months at a time and assumed a variety of characters. In one case, she played a fortune teller who pulled information from a superstitious suspect; in another, she befriended the wife of a suspected murderer and searched their home for clues. Pinkerton admitted, "She succeeded far beyond my utmost expectations, and I soon found her an invaluable acquisition to my force." Kate played an important role in some of Pinkerton's biggest cases, which occurred during a pivotal time in the nation's history.

Two years into her time at the agency, Kate was brought on to the Adams Express case. Adams Express was a postal delivery service akin to the Pony Express, and in 1858, several packages containing a total of $40,000 in cash (more than $1 million in today's money) went missing in Montgomery, Alabama. Employee Nathan Maroney was suspected, but there was no evidence, and several local private detectives had no luck solving the case. Finally, the company hired Pinkerton.

Kate went undercover as Madame Imbert, a sad, wealthy Southern woman whose dark secret was that her husband was in jail for forgery. (The character was named after an actual forger the Pinkertons had caught in a previous case.) Kate's goal was to observe and become friends with Nathan Maroney's wife. According to Pinkerton, "Kate Warne felt sure she was going to win. She always felt so, and I never knew her to be beaten." The way she gained Mrs. Maroney's trust was an art. Kate would pretend to weep over letters she received through the mail, but made a show of hiding her grief. This intrigued Mrs. Maroney, and she endeavored to befriend Madame Imbert. Slowly, Kate earned Mrs. Maroney's deepest trust. Soon, Mrs. Maroney was consulting Kate on the particulars of her husband's crime, how to handle the stolen money, and whether to trust her husband, who was in jail (but attempting to escape). Kate eventually convinced Mrs. Maroney to trust her with the money. Mrs. Maroney dug up the $40,000 up from the dirt cellar in her brother-in-law's house and handed it to Kate. As Pinkerton later wrote, "She had the proud satisfaction of knowing that to a woman belonged the honors of the day."

Kate believed a woman detective would be able to "go and worm out secrets in many places to which it was impossible for male detectives to gain access." Men, she explained, might not talk to their friends about their problems, but they turned to women to brag about their successes or to seek solace.

As Kate proved herself again and again, Pinkerton saw the value in hiring additional women detectives. Pinkerton made Kate the superintendent in charge of the new female detective bureau. Kate trained the new recruits, and as Pinkerton told them, "She has never let me down." Some of the women on Kate's forced included Hattie Lawton, who assisted key Pinkerton operative Timothy Webster in spying on the Confederacy; Vinnie Ream, a sculptor who kept an eye on the goings-on in the White House while working on a marble bust of Lincoln; and Mrs. E. H. Baker, who discovered Confederate plans for advanced weaponry that could've led to its ultimate victory had they not been discovered and destroyed.

A few years later, in 1861, Kate again participated in a high-profile Pinkerton case—this time involving president-elect Abraham Lincoln. After Lincoln's election but before he left his home in

Springfield, Illinois, for the White House, a railroad mechanic alerted Pinkerton to rumblings in Baltimore, Maryland, about an assassination plot. Lincoln planned to travel from Springfield to Washington, DC, via train, making stops in major towns along the way over several days, and the mechanic feared the assassination attempt might take place while Lincoln was on the train, as the route was public knowledge. Pinkerton and several of his men went undercover in Baltimore society as secessionists, hoping to gain entrance to the assassins' groups and learn of their plans. Kate went undercover as a Southern woman named Mrs. Barley sympathetic to secession. She wore a black-and-white rosette, which symbolized support for secession and was popular among the ladies of Baltimore, and she befriended the wives and daughters of the conspirators. In fact, Kate used her experience in the Adams Express case as background for this new character. Pinkerton wrote of her involvement in the early part of the case: "The information she received was invaluable. . . . Many hints were dropped in her presence which found their way to my ears, and were of great benefit to me."

One of Pinkerton's associates was able to earn the trust of the Baltimore police chief, from whom he learned that the city supported rebellion and the police were keeping an eye on those with Northern sympathies. The same associate helped Pinkerton gain entrance to one of the secret societies in Baltimore, which was led by an Italian anarchist, Cypriano Fernandina. At the meeting, Fernandina pulled out a knife and swore that Lincoln would not become president, that "if necessary, we will die together." The would-be assassins had not finalized their plan, but they hoped to use Lincoln's murder as an opportunity for secession.

Soon, the plan was settled: When Lincoln's train procession reached Baltimore in the middle of the day on February 23, they would distract those protecting Lincoln—with the support of the Baltimore police—and one of the men would use the opportunity to shoot him. Accomplices would help the assassin escape the city to Chesapeake Bay, where a steamer would be waiting to take the shooter to safety further south. The group had colleagues at every stop along Lincoln's route to telegraph (in code) if there were any changes to the time of his arrival.

With the exact plot uncovered, Pinkerton and his team moved full-steam ahead to stop it. He sent Kate to New York City to meet Lincoln's delegation and inform them of the plot. Meanwhile, he went to Philadelphia to prepare for Lincoln's arrival. When Lincoln's party reached Philadelphia the next day, Pinkerton met with Norman Judd, a former Illinois state senator who was part of Lincoln's team, and suggested that Lincoln go straight to Washington, DC, skipping the rest of his stops. Judd brought Pinkerton to Lincoln, who was dismayed but not scared. Lincoln told Pinkerton he was amenable to any plan that would allow him to fulfill his previously scheduled engagements in Philadelphia and Harrisburg the next day.

On February 22, 1861, on the train from Philadelphia to Harrisburg after Lincoln's event at Independence Hall, Pinkerton presented the plan. After the reception in Harrisburg was over, Lincoln would take a special 6 p.m. train, consisting only of one passenger car and one baggage car, back to Philadelphia. The 11 p.m. train from Philadelphia to Baltimore would be held until Lincoln's train from Harrisburg arrived, under the premise that Kate, undercover, was waiting for her invalid brother to arrive. Kate had secured the back half of a sleeping car, which had four berths: one for her, Pinkerton, Lincoln, and his personal bodyguard, Ward H. Lamon. It would be curtained off from the rest of the car so the other occupants would not realize who was back there. Kate's invalid brother was, of course, Lincoln himself, undercover wearing a hat and shawl. Pinkerton had coordinated with the American Telegraph Company to "fix" the telegraph lines leaving Harrisburg to prevent communication so no one in Baltimore could catch wind of the change in plans.

Once Lincoln and Lamon arrived at the Philadelphia train depot, Pinkerton wrote, "Mrs. Warne came forward, and familiarly greeting the president as her brother, we entered the sleeping car by the rear door without unnecessary delay, and without anyone being aware of the distinguished passenger who had arrived." Everyone in the party except Lincoln was armed with a pistol. Another of Pinkerton's men delivered a fake package to the conductor of the train—presumably the reason for the train being held up—and then it was off. No one outside Lincoln's inner circle knew he was on the train, including the train's conductor.

"The information Kate received was invaluable. . . . Many hints were dropped in her presence which found their way to my ears, and were of great benefit to me."

—Allan Pinkerton on Kate Warne

Pinkerton had his men stationed at several stops along the way to notify to him if anything changed. At Havre de Grace, Maryland, and every stop thereafter, Pinkerton got the signal that all was well. The train reached Baltimore at 3:30 a.m. and waited at the depot while Lincoln's sleeping car was transferred to another train, which went on to Washington, DC. Kate stayed behind in Baltimore to monitor the situation. Lincoln's train arrived at the crowded Washington depot at 6 a.m. Initially, Lincoln avoided recognition, but then Mr. Washburne of Illinois approached him. After a hand-shake, Pinkerton quickly staved him off. A carriage was waiting for Lincoln at the depot, which took him to Willard's Hotel on Pennsylvania Avenue. Lincoln had made it to Washington safely.

Later that day, Pinkerton returned to Baltimore, where many citizens were disappointed and angry to learn that Lincoln had made it to DC. Figuring their plan had come to light, the lead conspirators fled. Meanwhile, the rest of President Lincoln's party, including Mrs. Lincoln, arrived in Baltimore as originally scheduled. One of Pinkerton's men in Harrisburg had spilled the beans about the plot to the press. Of course, the plot wasn't published until after Lincoln had safely arrived in Washington—the malfunction-ing telegraph lines had made that certain—but the press wrote all about Baltimore.

As Lincoln's first term progressed into the Civil War, Pinkerton became the head of a new government agency: the Secret Service. For a time, he placed Kate undercover in the South, likely in Tennessee. Her fake identity was that of a Southern belle, and she gained information on the Confederacy by befriending other Southern women and flirting with Southern men. She even interacted with John Wilkes Booth. She played a similar role undercover in Maryland, Virginia, and DC, where she got to know the female secessionists of the area's elite families. At another point, she and Pinkerton posed as a married couple. She continued as the head of Pinkerton's female department of detectives throughout the Civil War, where many of her operatives did courageous work, equal in their fearlessness to any of their male counterparts.

Sadly, Kate's career didn't continue long past the Civil War. On January 28, 1868, she died from pneumonia after a month-long illness. She was around 35 years old and had worked as a detective for about 12 years. Her employer and friend Allan Pinkerton was by her side as she passed, and he had her buried in his family plot in Graceland Cemetery in Chicago near her colleague Timothy Webster, who was executed by the Confederacy during the war after he was discovered to be a Union spy. Pinkerton and his wife were later buried nearby.

About a decade after Kate's death, some of Pinkerton's top male agents asked him to reconsider his policy on hiring women detectives. Apparently, their wives weren't comfortable with them working alongside women. Many also claimed the job was too dangerous for women—perhaps because the accomplishments of female detectives during the Civil War were no longer in recent memory or perhaps because Pinkerton had not yet documented them in his many memoirs. But Pinkerton stood his ground to anyone who questioned the reasoning behind his female detective bureau and often cited Kate as the example that proved his point.

Pinkerton's innovation in hiring Kate led the way not only for the other women detectives in his own agency, but also for all women in law enforcement and investigation. Other organizations took their time following Pinkerton's lead: The first woman wasn't allowed to join the NYPD until 1891, and the department didn't hire a woman detective until 1903.

Peseshet
(c. 2400 BCE)

In the Old Kingdom of ancient Egypt, sometime between the Fourth and Sixth Dynasties, lived the first known female physician, Peseshet. We know about her from the excavation of the Giza tomb of her son, Akhet-Hetep, who had many roles serving the Pharaoh. In the tomb, a white-limestone *stela* (stone slab dedicated to a deceased person) describes Peseshet as *imy-r swnwt*, which translates to "overseer of physicians." The *t* indicates the female gender and has caused scholars to argue whether she was the female overseer of male physicians or the female overseer of female physicians, and whether she was also a physician, but it seems unlikely that a woman would be in charge of physicians without being one herself. Part of her role as chief physician was serving the pharaoh's mother.

Peseshet was also overseer of funerary priestesses in charge of funerary rites, which, with embalming, were connected to medicine. She likely came from a wealthy family to have reached this privileged position and probably practiced during the time of the Great Pyramids' construction.

It's interesting to note the similarity between Peseshet's name and the word *peseshkef*, which was an ancient Egyptian knife used to cut the umbilical cord. According to the *stela*, Peseshet lived until "a very good old age." The next known woman doctor was not for several thousand more years, in the Ptolemaic period (305–30 BCE).

FUNMILAYO RANSOME-KUTI

(1900–1978)

As one of the first girls to ever to attend her elementary school, the first Nigerian woman to drive a car, the first African woman to visit China, and the first woman to found a Nigerian political party, Funmilayo Ransome-Kuti lived a life full of firsts that would pave the way for others.

Frances Abigail Olufunmilayo Thomas was born on October 25, 1900, in Abeokuta, a once-autonomous kingdom that was then part of the British-ruled colonial protectorate of Southern Nigeria. Her parents were Lucretia Phyllis Morenke Dese, a dressmaker, and Daniel Olumoyewa Thomas, a farmer and palm oil trader. Both were Christians educated in missionary schools who retained ties to their Yoruba culture. Funmilayo's paternal great-grandmother had been a returned slave (freed by British anti-slavery patrol ships), and her paternal grandfather was one of the first Christians in Abeokuta after missionaries came to the area in the 1840s. At the time, his religion was a marker of more elite members of Abeokuta society.

Funmilayo's parents supported educating girls, which was still uncommon in the early 1900s. Her parents sent her to missionary schools until 1914, when she became one of the first girls enrolled at the Abeokuta Grammar School, which was built by the Abeokuta District Council, separate from the British government or missionaries. Funmilayo's formative high school years were spent watching Great Britain tighten its grip on her home.

In 1919, Funmilayo's parents sent her to England to continue her education at Wincham Hall School for Girls in Cheshire. She studied elocution, domestic science, and music, but she also faced intense racism. Although the opportunity to study in England was the sign of extreme privilege in her Abeokuta community, it ultimately brought her closer to her Yoruba roots and spurred her anti-colonial politics. Upon returning to Abeokuta in 1922, she dropped her English name and went exclusively by her Yoruba name, Funmilayo. Soon after her return, she began teaching at Abeokuta Grammar School.

On January 20, 1925, Funmilayo was married to Reverend Israel Oludotun Ransome-Kuti, who was also from an educated Christian family. She was 25 years old, and he was 34. It's possible she met her future husband at Abeokuta Grammar School when she was still a student and he was a teacher. When they married, he was the principal of a school in a neighboring town, the Ijebu-Ode Grammar School, and Funmilayo left Abeokuta and joined her husband, known to his friends as Daodu, in Ijebu-Ode.

During her time there, Funmilayo set up a club for the elite young women of Ijebu-Ode society, with the goal of socialization and self-improvement. She started a nursery school and a series of literacy classes for lower-class women who sold goods in the markets. Additionally, she and Daodu were among the founders of the Nigerian chapter of the West African Students Union, an anti-colonialist organization founded in London in 1925. In 1926, Funmilayo gave birth to her first child, a daughter, Dolupo, who was followed by a son, Olikoye, two years later.

In 1932, Daodu was hired as the new principal of Abeokuta Grammar School. Around the same time, Daodu cofounded the Nigerian Union of Teachers, of which he was also president. Funmilayo brought what she'd learned in Ijebu-Ode to her hometown, establishing the Abeokuta Ladies Club (ALC) for educated Christian women to "raise the standard of womanhood in Abeokuta." Daodu was a strong supporter of the ALC. The couple lived an upper-middle-class life in Abeokuta; they resided on a large compound and raised livestock. They were the first family in town to own a car, and Funmilayo was reportedly the first Nigerian woman to drive. Theirs was a marriage of support and mutual respect. Funmilayo gave birth to their third child, Fela, on October 15, 1938, and their youngest, Beko, in about 1941.

In 1944, the ALC broadened its membership and began admitting market women, shifting its elitist reputation and political direction. The ALC held literacy classes for market women, and Funmilayo discovered that government officials were confiscating their rice, then selling it themselves and keeping the profits. The ALC protested this practice at press conferences. Around the same time, Funmilayo decided to stop wearing Western clothing and dress only in Yoruba traditional garb to further decolonize herself and align with the market women. The following year, in 1946, the Abeokuta Ladies Club changed its name to the Abeokuta Women's Union (AWU), keeping Funmilayo as president. This change reflected the political goals of the organization, which hoped to advanced the place of all women in Abeokuta society, not just educated Christians. The group had its own constitution, which reflected its goals to become more inclusive to all. The native Yoruba language—not English—was the primary language of the club, and traditional Yoruba dress was encouraged. Education was also a core value, as it was seen as a way to improve the lives of all women in society. Funmilayo worked to bring market women into the AWU's leadership. Soon, the AWU had an estimated membership of 20,000.

Funmilayo set up a club for the elite young women of Ijebu-Ode society, with the goal of socialization and self-improvement. She started a nursery school and a series of literacy classes for lower-class women who sold goods in the markets.

Starting sometime in 1946, Funmilayo and the AWU focused on the unfair taxation placed on women. Since 1918, the colonial government had taxed the genders differently, specifically targeting market women and cloth-dyers, who were successful entrepreneurs and vital to the economy. The enforcement was especially cruel: Tax collectors sometimes determined whether a girl was old enough to pay taxes by stripping her naked to see if she had developed breasts. The colonial government also implemented controls on what goods market women could sell, as well as how they could price those items. Other parts of the Nigerian Protectorate did not tax their women citizens so aggressively. The local head of the British authorities was the sovereign ruler, *Alake*, Ademola II, and he directed the enforcement of these rules. This brought the into question larger issue of power under colonialism, as the market women were being taxed, but had no representation in the country's political structure. In public forums, Funmilayo spoke to authorities only in Yoruba and insisted that their English replies be translated. Over several months, Funmilayo and the AWU tried traditional forms of protest, like petitions. When they had no success, they stepped up their game.

In early 1947, Funmilayo refused to pay her taxes and was arrested as a result. About 8,000 women protested outside her arraignment, and 5,000 more were at her trial a week later. She was ordered to pay a £3 fine. This was just the beginning. Other women refused to pay their taxes, and sit-ins and mass protests became the norm. In November 1947, a crowd of 10,000 women stormed the Alake's compound, singing protest songs about the injustices they faced: "Ibadan womenfolk do not pay any tax/Lagos women do not pay any tax/What sins have the Egba women committed to warrant the imposition of taxation?" A month later, the women held another demonstration, where they expanded their demands to include the abdication of the Alake. The press was supportive as the protests continued. In April 1948, a march through the streets of Abeokuta finally accomplished their initial goal: to end the direct taxation of women. The women weren't done, however. On January 3, 1949, they succeeded in getting the Alake to abdicate his rule and forced him into exile.

With their major success against the Alake, in 1949 the Abeokuta Women's Union expanded to a national organization, the Nigerian Women's Union (NWU). Funmilayo remained the organization's president, with the aim to do for all Nigerian woman what she had for those of Abeokuta. She said in a June 1949 speech on the state of womanhood: "There is no country that can rise above her womenfolk." The NWU brought together women across Nigeria, despite language and cultural differences, to advocate for women's representation in government and the right to vote. In 1953, the NWU evolved into the Federation of Nigerian Women Societies, whose mission was "to liberate women socially, educationally, culturally, economically, and politically." Funmilayo did not align the organization with any specific political parties so it had the freedom and flexibility to best represent women's interests.

In the early 1940s, Daodu helped found the Nigerian Union of Students in addition to his Nigerian Union of Teachers. In August 1944, the organization initiated a protest against the colonial government's policies on education. Daodu and Funmilayo helped form a new political party, the National Council of Nigeria and the Cameroons (NCNC).

During the time of the tax protests in 1947, Funmilayo was also involved in negotiations around the new Nigerian constitution. As part of an NCNC delegation, she was the lone woman in a group of seven who traveled to London to present a petition of protest regarding the proposed Richards Constitution, which was not debated in Nigeria. Despite the delegation's efforts, the constitution went into effect, but the complaints were noted, and in 1949, the new governor of the colony, Sir John Macpherson, called for regional conferences to discuss a new constitution. Funmilayo was the only woman present at the Western Regional Conference, where she voiced concern for women's rights, including suffrage.

While she was in London in 1947, Funmilayo contacted women's groups in the United Kingdom and interacted with the press, including the BBC. She wrote an article for the *Daily Worker* called "We Had Equality 'til Britain Came," which forcefully voiced anti-colonial sentiments. This piece drew attention to Funmilayo on the international stage—including from the Women's International Democratic Federation (WIDF), a French socialist organization that was expanding globally. In 1953, when the Nigerian Women's Union evolved into the Federation of Nigerian Women Societies, it was aligned with the global WIDF, of which Funmilayo was elected vice president.

"There is no country that can rise above her womenfolk."

Daodu passed away in 1955 at the age of 64. The couple had been married for 30 years. His death may have sparked the vigor with which Funmilayo threw herself into her role as vice president of the WIDF. On behalf of the organization, she visited the countries of the Eastern Bloc during the late 1950s and early 1960s: Bulgaria, the Soviet Union, Hungary, Poland, Yugoslavia, and East Germany. She was the first African woman to visit most of these nations. In 1956, she was the first African woman to visit China, meeting with Chairman Mao Tse-tung about women's rights in communist China. Everywhere she traveled, she joined local women's groups and global humanitarian organizations. Even though she never identified as a communist, the Nigerian and British government did not approve of her travels. Neither did the United States: When Funmilayo wanted to visit and meet with African-American leaders in the United States in the 1950s, she was denied an entry visa. In 1957, Nigerian Prime Minister Tafawa Balewa personally refused to renew Funmilayo's passport; however, when Nigeria won its independence from Great Britain in 1960, her passport was renewed.

With independence came suffrage for most women in Nigeria, but northern Nigerian women had to wait until 1977. Funmilayo continued advocating for them after independence. Funmilayo had been running for office through the NCNC for years. The first time was in 1951, when she lost an election for a seat on the regional assembly (although she was the only woman candidate to get past the first stage). She wanted to run again in 1959, but the NCNC rejected her bid, so she broke with the party and ran as an independent. She was then expelled from the NCNC—which was fine with her, as she no longer agreed with their policies—and she became the first Nigerian woman to form her own political party, the Commoners' People's Party, which lasted only a year.

Funmilayo's political life began to slow down as Nigeria moved into a period of successive military coups and regimes. She began collecting awards in recognition of her lifetime of advocacy. In 1965, the Nigerian government named Funmilayo a Member of the Order of the Niger in honor of her great contributions to the country. Three years later, she was given an honorary doctorate from the University of Ibadan, and in 1970, she was awarded the Lenin Peace Prize (the Soviet equivalent of a Nobel Peace Prize) for her work promoting friendship between the Nigerian and Soviet people.

She spent most of this time with her adult children, with whom she'd grown closer than ever. She and Daodu had been strict parents. Fela later recalled: "I don't think anybody kicked my ass as much as my mother. But I dug her. I liked to hear her talk, discuss. . . . I vaguely remember when she started getting into politics. . . . Because when she was running around doing politics she didn't have time to flog me." Music was nearly as big a part of their household as activism. Daodu was a musician, and there was a piano in their home. Young Fela showed a gift for music, and in 1958, with Beko's help, Fela persuaded Funmilayo to send him to Trinity College of Music in London. He would experience much of the same racism Funmilayo had faced decades earlier, and he returned to Nigeria equally radicalized, becoming famous for his songs about injustice. He had an ally in his mother, who had raised her children to become fierce activists.

All of the Kuti clan were vocal opponents of the military governments that characterized Nigerian politics in the late 1960s and 1970s. In the early 1970s, when Fela changed his last name to Anikulapo-Kuti to get rid of the European-rooted Ransome, Funmilayo changed hers as well. She also moved in with Fela at the compound he'd made out of her land near Lagos on Agege Motor Road, which he deemed the Kalakuta Republic. In 1977, about 1,000 soldiers raided the compound. In the course of the attack, items were broken and stolen, inhabitants were beaten and raped, and Funmilayo was thrown out of a second-story window. She never recovered from her injuries, and died on April 13, 1978. She was 77 years old.

Nigerian newspapers mourned her death, calling her "the defender of women's rights." Fela responded by releasing the album *Unknown Soldier* in 1979, containing the eponymous 30-minute song in which he describes the raid in detail. In the song, he calls Funmilayo "the only mother of Nigeria." The following year, he released *Coffin for Head of State*, describing how, following her death, he brought Funmilayo's coffin to the gate of the army barracks to display what they'd done. Funmilayo's children donated her papers to the University of Ibadan Library, but she is best remembered for their work as activists, and Fela's as an activist-musician.

EUNICE NEWTON FOOTE

(1819–1888)

There were one hundred signatures on the Declaration of Sentiments at the first Women's Rights Convention in Seneca Falls, New York. The fifth signature, just after Elizabeth Cady Stanton, belonged to Eunice Newton Foote. Eunice was a revolutionary thinker and scientist who only recently began to receive attention for her landmark discovery: the greenhouse effect and the possibility of climate change.

Eunice was born on July 17, 1819, in Connecticut. Her family moved to Troy, New York, north of Albany. Upstate New York was a haven for liberal philosophies such as abolition, suffrage, and temperance. Eunice attended the Troy Female Seminary, which was unusual because it allowed its female students to take science classes at a local men's college. The college, called the Rensselaer School, was started by Amos Eaton, an early advocate for women's education. Eunice learned the basics of scientific experimentation at the Rensselaer School, and while at Troy Female Seminary, she studied with Almira Hart Lincoln Phelps, a groundbreaking female scientist.

In 1841, at age 22, Eunice married Elisha Foote, a lawyer who had recently finished his legal studies under Judge Daniel Cady, father of soon-to-be-famous suffragist Elizabeth Cady Stanton. Nothing is known of Eunice and Elisha's courtship or how the two met, but they were undoubtedly a well-matched couple in an almost modern sense. They shared an interest in science, and they likely collaborated on experiments in the laboratory they set up in their home in Seneca Falls, New York. On July 21, 1842, Eunice gave birth to the couple's first child, Mary, and two years later, on October 24, 1844, she had their second daughter, Augusta. Elisha became district attorney for Seneca County and served as village president in the 1840s.

Eunice's next-door neighbor in Seneca Falls was Elizabeth Cady Stanton. The women became friends. The details of Eunice's involvement in the early suffrage movement are unknown, but both Eunice and Elisha were present at the first Women's Rights Convention in Seneca Falls in July 1848. There, the Declaration of Sentiments written by Cady Stanton—which demanded women's equality and the right to vote—was presented and signed by 100 participants. The completed declaration held the signatures of 68 women and 32 men, including Elisha and Frederick Douglass. Eunice was one of only five women (including Cady Stanton) named to the editorial committee "to prepare the proceedings of the Convention for publication." The editorial committee collaborated with Douglass, who oversaw the printing of the convention proceedings and published both the proceedings and the minutes in his newspaper, *The North Star*.

Eunice and Elisha's amateur scientific experiments reached their pinnacle in 1856. They each concluded studies—possibly conducted in coordination—and published papers on their findings in *The American Journal of Science and Arts*. They attended the meeting of the American Association for the Advancement of Science (AAAS) on August 23, 1856, in Albany, New York, to present their research. Neither Eunice nor Elisha was a member of the association, although Elisha joined the after the meeting, which was the largest to date. Eunice's findings were presented by Professor Joseph Henry, the founding director of the Smithsonian Institute. Historians have speculated that Eunice did not make the presentation because women weren't allowed or because colleagues typically presented on behalf of one another.

Professor Henry introduced Eunice's work, "Circumstances Affecting the Heat of Sun's Rays," by saying, "Science [is] of no country and of no sex. The sphere of woman embraces not only the beautiful and the useful, but the true." He then went on to explain the procedures and findings of Eunice's experiments. She took two glass cylinders, one with "condensed air" (with more carbon dioxide, then called carbonic acid) and the other with "exhausted air" (with less carbon dioxide). She then measured the temperatures inside the cylinders as she left them out in the sun. She found the air with more carbon dioxide rose to 20 degrees higher than the air with less carbon dioxide and took much longer to cool when removed from the sun. She also tested the effect of heat on moist air versus dry air and on hydrogen versus oxygen. Eunice concluded: "An atmosphere of that gas would give to our earth a much higher temperature; and if there once was, as some suppose, a larger proportion of that gas in the air, an increased temperature must have accompanied it."

Eunice had studied the warming effects of carbon dioxide in the atmosphere. In other words, she discovered the greenhouse effect and the potential for global warming—in 1856.

It's unknown how Eunice's research was received at the conference. The following month, a column in *Scientific American* titled

"Scientific Ladies—Experiments with Condensed Gases" highlighted Eunice's work, citing her as proof that women were more than capable of participating in scientific research: "The experiments of Mrs. Foot[e] afford abundant evidence of the ability of a woman to investigate any subject with originality and precision." Eunice's page-and-a-half paper was published in November 1856.

Curiously, the very same issue featured an article on color blindness by well-known Irish scientist John Tyndall, who was blunt in his belief that women were intellectually inferior to men. Three years later, in 1859, Tyndall published a paper in the *Proceedings of the Royal Society of London* detailing his (more complex) experiments proving the heat-trapping effects of carbon dioxide and water vapor. Since then, Tyndall has been credited as the father of climate science, while no discussion of Eunice's findings before the 21st century has ever been found.

In August 1857, Eunice presented another paper, "On a New Source of Electrical Excitement," to the AAAS in Montreal. In her presentation, she described how, over the course of eight months of experimentation, she observed the effects of compression and expansion in the atmosphere on the air's electricity. Her paper was published in 1858. Because evidence of discussion of her work has not been found, it's unknown if her findings helped further science's understanding of the relationship between barometric pressure and electricity.

Eunice had studied the warming effects of carbon dioxide in the atmosphere. In other words, she discovered the greenhouse effect and the potential for global warming—in 1856.

Eunice's scientific interests also resulted in the patents of several inventions, including one in 1860 for "filling for soles of boots and shoes." Elisha was also entrepreneurial and, fittingly, specialized in patent law. He also had a passion for mathematics and published a book on calculus. Several of his patents made a considerable amount of money, including an automatic draft regulator for stoves. That particular invention was the subject of several lawsuits and went all the way to the Supreme Court, where Elisha argued on his own behalf.

When Elisha was appointed to the Board of Appeals at the US Patent Office in 1864, the Foote family moved from Saratoga Springs, New York, where they'd raised and educated their daughters, to Washington, DC. Eunice and Elisha's older daughter, Mary, met Senator John B. Henderson from Missouri, whom she married in June 1868. The senator was one of the authors of the Thirteenth Amendment, which ended slavery. Elisha served as the US Commissioner of Patents from 1868 to 1869. Once his term was over, he went back to patent law, and it's thought that the couple moved back to Saratoga Springs.

Elisha died in October 1883 at age 74. Eunice and Elisha had been married for more than 40 years. Eunice died in fall 1888 at 69 years old. Her cause of death, like much of her later life, is unknown, and the exact date of her death is disputed. She's buried in Brooklyn, New York, at Green-Wood Cemetery.

More than 150 years after her experiments proved the effects of greenhouse gases, Eunice's work was resurrected thanks to a serendipitous discovery by independent researcher Raymond Sorenson. He was perusing his collection of old scientific books and documents when he found the 1857 proceedings of the AAAS meeting. What he read didn't jibe with the accepted history of climate science. In 2011, he wrote a paper on Eunice's work, and since then, research on Eunice's life and research has started to emerge. In December 2019, Sotheby's auctioned off a first printing of her article, estimating its value at $2,000 to $3,000. The lot sold for $4,750, a sign that her contributions to history are at long last being recognized.

Acknowledgments

I weirdly love reading the acknowledgments section at the end of books and the special thanks at the end of movies, so it's thrilling to write one myself.

Thank you to my editor and friend Morgan Shanahan, who championed a first-time author and without whom this book would not exist. To everyone else at Callisto Media: Alexandra Asher Sears, Erin Yeung, Martin Worthington, and Sigi Nacson—it was truly a team effort to get this book across the finish line, so thank you. I'm eternally grateful.

To my family for truly everything, but especially my brother, Aaron, for his technical assistance. To my pals who kept in touch, kept me sane, and sent me memes when I cut myself off from the world to finish this: Gaby Grossman, Annie Jeong, Mike Halpern (who went so far as to screen-record can't-miss moments like Oprah singing "Shallow" from *A Star Is Born*), Briana Byrd, and Becca Sita. To my lifetime BFFs RW/Deep Thoughts: Vidya Kulavil, Nicole Pyon, Rachel Chang, Michelle Chan, and Yoshimi Yoshida. You guys are my constants and my safe space. To my London girls: Alexa Keane, Monica Ball, Caroline (Miller) Gahl, and Maggie Daly, who shaped me into a responsible human being. To the near-commune of families who raised me, especially the Maiers and Nakatas.

Thank you to the Boston University libraries and the Los Angeles Public Library for access to their resources.

To the OG research crew: Mariana Uribe (to whom I owe my entire adult life), Leo Chiquillo, and Leena Gundapaneni, and to the research coven: Micki Taylor, Rachel Schnalzer, Lauren Woelfel, and Alaina Rook—we finally got Kate Warne in something, gang!

About the Author

Kari Koeppel is a writer and editor who graduated from Boston University before returning to her native Los Angeles. She was an early hire to BuzzFeed's video research department, where she helped create accurate, engaging content for millions of viewers, culminating in a multifaceted role as head of research, copy, and quality control. Her writing has appeared in BuzzFeed, McSweeney's, and this book, which is her first. She tweets about film and feminism at @karikoeppel.

CPSIA information can be obtained
at www.ICGtesting.com
Printed in the USA
JSHW041916120222
22846JS00002B/4